HISTORICAL ATLAS OF NEW MEXICO

HISTORICAL ATLAS OF NEW MEXICO

University of Oklahoma Press : Norman

HISTORICAL ATLAS
OF NEW MEXICO

BY
WARREN A. BECK
AND
YNEZ D. HAASE

Library of Congress Catalog Card Number: 68-31366

ISBN: 0-8061-0817-7

Copyright © 1969 by the University of Oklahoma Press, Publishing Division of the University. Manufactured in the U.S.A. First edition, 1969; second printing, 1976; third printing, 1979; fourth printing, 1985.

PREFACE

NEW MEXICO HAS HAD a long and eventful history. It was the scene of a very large population in prehistoric times, and many Indians made it their home before the Spaniards first came in 1541. A sizable number of Hispanic people made it their home when the Anglos came in 1846. The history of the state is the story of the blending of its Indian, Hispanic, and Anglo societies.

Its vast size, its location in the Southwest, and its varied geography have all influenced New Mexico's history. To understand this interrelationship of geography with history adequately, it is necessary to know the geography of the state, the location of population concentration through the years, the routes followed by explorer, conqueror, trader, and settler, the development of frontier posts and forts, the land system and boundaries of the state, and, finally, the state's economic development. An effort has been made to show on maps the places that have played a significant role in New Mexico's history. Some selection was necessary, as not all could be included. On the page opposite each map a brief account describing the map or what it represents is provided.

The spellings of the Indian names in use at the time the map represents have been followed. The names of places are those current at the time represented by the map. The names did change from time to time; and, consequently, different spellings or even slightly different names appear. With a few exceptions, accent marks are no longer used.

The maps in the atlas are numbered consecutively. All numbers in the index are map numbers; there are no page numbers in the map section of the book.

Of the many who have contributed to the preparation of this historical atlas special thanks are due the following: the State Museum and State Archivist of New Mexico, the Bureau of Land Management in Santa Fe, the Department of Agricultural Economics at New Mexico State University, and the library staffs of the University of New Mexico, California State College at Fullerton, and the Huntington Library, San Marino, California.

The authors sincerely hope that this atlas will be of help to all those interested in the exciting history of New Mexico. We have labored to develop an atlas that will aid the professional scholar but will also make it possible for amateur historians, as well as students at the secondary and college levels, to better understand the historical-geographical relationships upon which the state of New Mexico has developed.

WARREN A. BECK
YNEZ D. HAASE

CONTENTS

HISTORICAL ATLAS OF NEW MEXICO

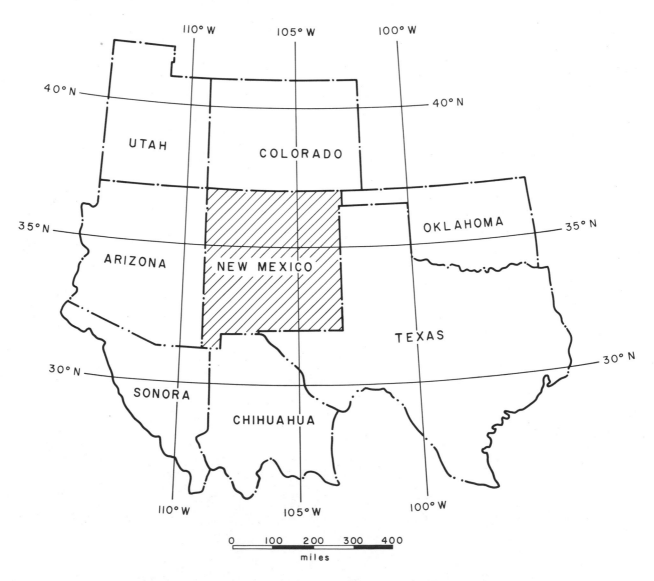

LOCATION OF NEW MEXICO

1. LOCATION OF NEW MEXICO

NEW MEXICO IS LOCATED in the southwestern part of the United States, between 103° and 109° West Longitude, and 32° and 37° North Latitude. The state has a common boundary with Colorado on the north, Oklahoma and Texas on the east, Texas and Mexico on the south, and Arizona on the west. The northwestern corner of the state touches corners of Arizona, Colorado, and Utah. This is the only place in the United States where four states meet.

New Mexico is the fifth-largest state in the Union, having a total land area of 121,666 square miles. Its water area, however, covers 155 square miles, less than in any other state. Except for the slight panhandle at the southwest corner, the state is almost a perfect rectangle. It measures 390 miles from north to south and 350 miles from east to west.

The latitudinal location of New Mexico, plus its great size, has had a marked influence on the cultural activities of its inhabitants. Some authorities classify it as a southwestern state, although others regard it as one of the Rocky Mountain states. Actually, the eastern one-third of the state is geographically an extension of Texas, and the rest is mountain terrain. Most of the state is in the drier western part of the nation, only certain mountain areas receiving adequate rainfall. The isolation from the rest of the nation that determined much of the history of New Mexico has been virtually eliminated since the advent of the railroad, the automobile, and—more recently—the airplane. The state's proximity to Mexico and its large native Hispanic population have influenced its culture tremendously.

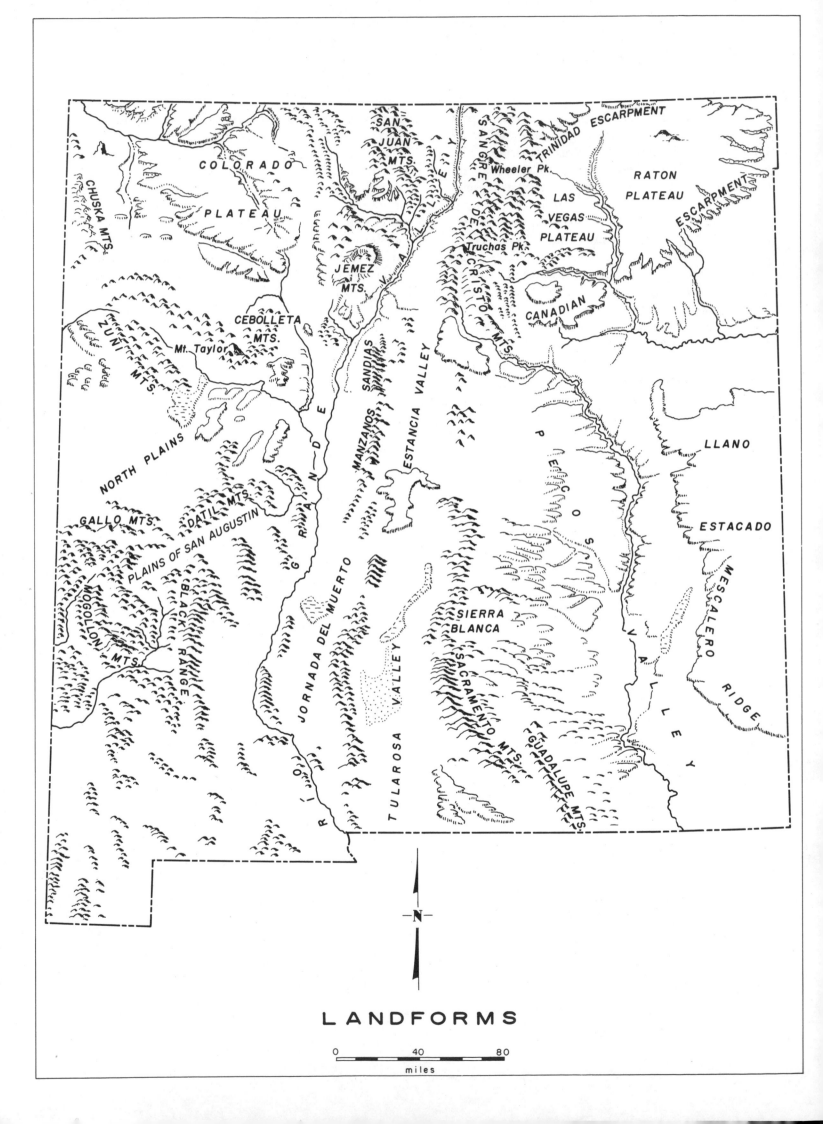

CHUSKA MTS.

COLORADO
PLATEAU

SAN
JUAN
MTS.

TRINIDAD ESCARPMENT

Wheeler Pk.

RATON
PLATEAU

ESCARPMENT

LAS
VEGAS
PLATEAU

JEMEZ
MTS.

Truchas Pk.

CEBOLLETA
MTS.

Mt. Taylor

ZUNI MTS.

SANDIAS

MANZANOS

CANADIAN

NORTH PLAINS

ESTANCIA VALLEY

P E C O S

LLANO

GALLO MTS.

DATIL MTS.

PLAINS OF SAN AUGUSTIN

MOGOLLON MTS.

BLACK RANGE

JORNADA DEL MUERTO

TULAROSA VALLEY

ESTACADO

SIERRA
BLANCA

SACRAMENTO MTS.

GUADALUPE MTS.

V A L L E Y

MESCALERO RIDGE

SANGRE DE CRISTO MTS.

R I O   G R A N D E

N

LANDFORMS

0   40   80
miles

2. LANDFORMS

THE NEW MEXICO LANDSCAPE has several high mountain peaks; the highest are Wheeler Peak and Truchas Peak in the Sangre de Cristo Range, which rise to 13,160 feet and 13,100 feet, respectively. The state's mountain ranges and major divides run in a north-south direction, but with some variations. In general, the state is an altiplano with 85 per cent of the area having an elevation over 4,000 feet. The southeast corner is some 3,000 feet above sea level, while the northwest corner is 5,305 feet.

Landforms in New Mexico are complex because they include parts of the Rockies and the Great Plains, in addition to plateaus, basins, and ranges. Two splinters of the Rockies intrude into the state. The San Juan and Jemez Mountains make up the western splinter; the Sangre de Cristo Mountains make up the eastern one. The Sangre de Cristos are a tilted block of crystalline rocks, whereas the western mountains are of volcanic origin. A plateau about 140 miles wide separates the two ranges.

To the east of the Sangre de Cristos are two concentric scarps: the Trinidad and the Canadian. The Trinidad bounds a plateau that has been so eroded that there is little flat surface left. The Canadian Escarpment, the lower plateau, has sharply entrenched valleys and numerous mesas capped by layers of lava. The Llano Estacado, south of the Canadian Escarpment, includes some of the flattest surface in the world.

West of the San Juan and Jemez Mountains is a portion of the Colorado Plateau. This region has nearly horizontal sedimentary rocks carved into a gentle relief of broad mesas and valleys. The Zuñi Mountains are at the southern edge of the Colorado Plateau in the form of an elongated dome. Just east of this dome but at right angles to it are the Cebolleta Mountains, made of basaltic lava (Mt. Taylor, 11,289 feet high, being the prominent peak).

South of the Cebolletas are the North Plains, an elongated depression occupied partly by alluvium and partly by a young lava field. Farther south and similar to the North Plains are the Plains of San Augustin. Between these two areas and still farther south are masses of volcanic rocks which make up the Datil, Gallinas, Gallo, and Mogollon Mountains.

Within New Mexico are many alluvial basins which have been very important in developing the state's agriculture. Very little of the alluvium has been laid down by the state's streams, since they are mainly confined to well-entrenched canyons. Instead, the alluvial plains are found between the mountains, having been formed by materials washed down from the uplifted rim over a very long period of time.

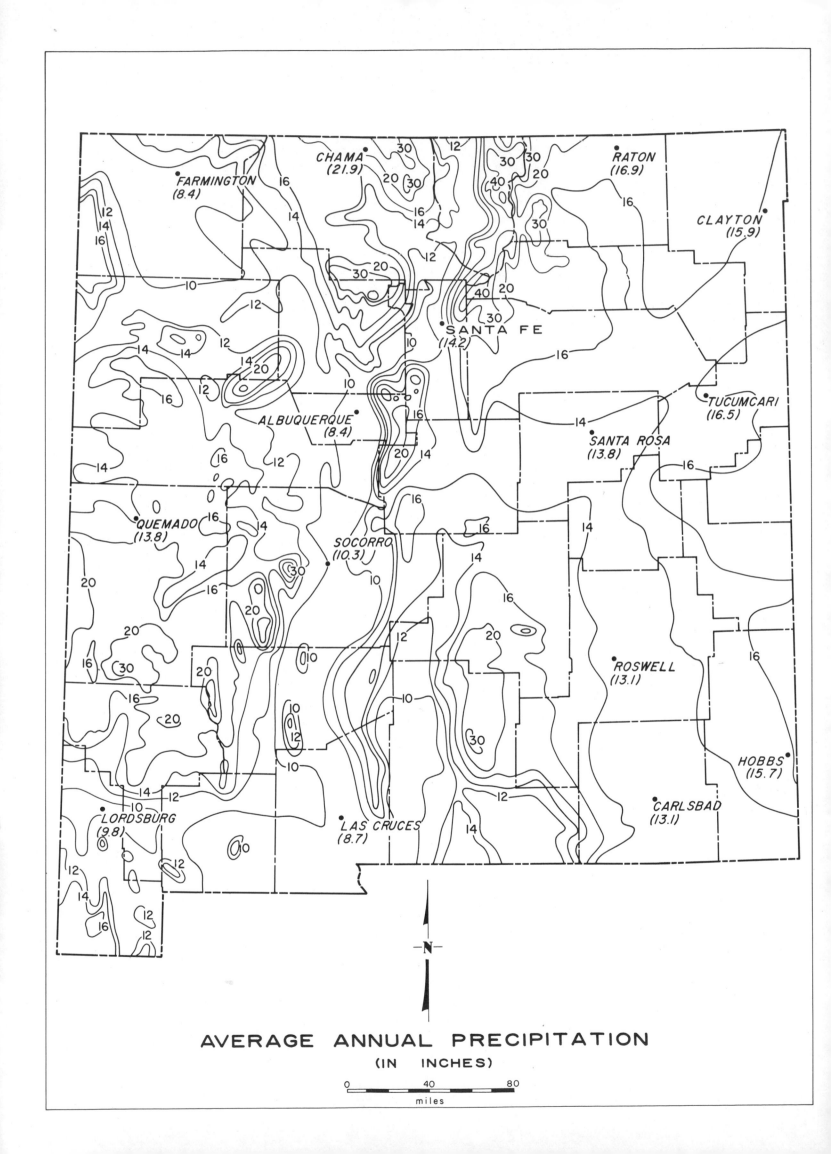

AVERAGE ANNUAL PRECIPITATION

(IN INCHES)

3. AVERAGE ANNUAL PRECIPITATION

THE AVERAGE ANNUAL RAINFALL in New Mexico is 15 inches. Normally, precipitation increases with elevation, particularly along the New Mexico Rocky Mountains. A high of 40 inches of rainfall is reached in the upper parts of the Jemez and Sangre de Cristo Mountains. The drier portions of New Mexico which receive only 8 to 10 inches of rainfall a year are the basin areas of the San Juan and Chaco rivers, the Río Grande Valley south of Española, the southern part of the Tularosa Valley, and the area known as Jornada del Muerto. In general, precipitation is greatest in the eastern third of the state and least in the western portion. This is true because the source of most New Mexico moisture is the Gulf of Mexico, and the farther one goes from that body, the less precipitation.

Most of the precipitation in the state comes in the form of local high-intensity storms of relatively short duration. Such storms result when warm moist Gulf air moves inland and becomes unstable over the hot terrain, causing heavy thundershowers. These usually occur in late afternoon and are especially common in the southern slope of the Rockies. Fortunately, most of the rain falls from June to September, when it will do the most good. Unfortunately, like in most steppe semiarid climatic regions, New Mexico's rainfall is notoriously unreliable. Throughout the history of the state, droughts have been the principal plague of the land. Many observers contend that droughts have caused groups of Indians to abandon the land. Parts of the state have suffered catastrophic drought the very same year that other sections of the state have received rainfall in excess of the average. Rainfall statistics, however, do not always tell the full story. Sometimes drought has resulted when more than average rain has fallen; but, in other years, even with precipitation less than average, there has been adequate rainfall for both crops and grass. The explanation for this seeming paradox is that rainfall frequently occurs in torrential downpours. Several inches may fall in a single day, leaving the land flooded and crops seriously damaged. Naturally, if the showers occur more frequently, they are more beneficial, even if much less moisture is recorded.

Snow falls in every part of the state. The amount varies with latitude and elevation, from 2 to 5 inches in the Río Grande Valley up to 300 inches in the mountains. About three-fourths of the annual streamflow originates in forest and grassland regions above 8,000 feet, where the snowfall is more than half the annual precipitation. The accumulation of snow in the mountains largely determines the amount of water available for irrigation during the growing season.

The value of the total rainfall in any given area is determined by temperature conditions. During the summer season, when temperatures frequently exceed 90° F., large amounts of water that could otherwise be used for crop production are lost by evaporation. Moisture in the mountain areas where temperatures are lower obviously goes farther in the production of crops and grasslands.

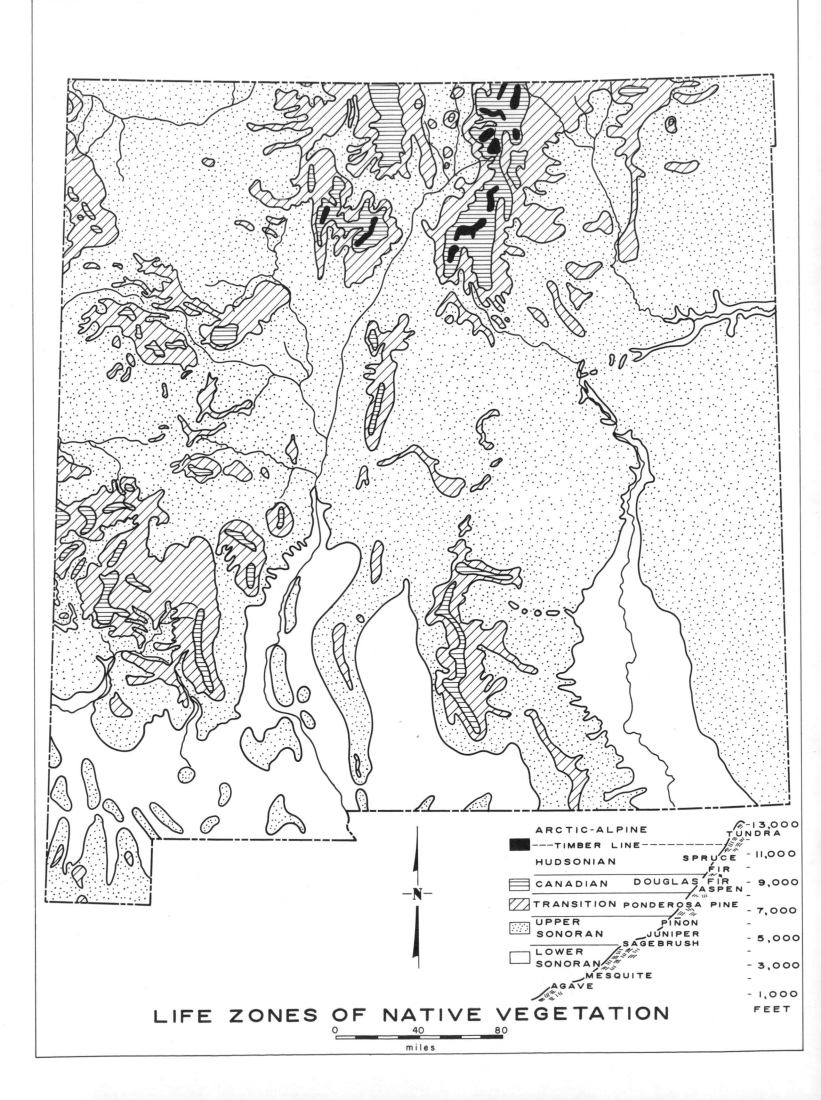

ARCTIC-ALPINE ⎯13,000
TUNDRA
■ ⎯⎯TIMBER LINE⎯⎯
HUDSONIAN SPRUCE ⎯11,000
FIR
CANADIAN DOUGLAS FIR ⎯9,000
ASPEN
TRANSITION PONDEROSA PINE ⎯7,000
UPPER PIÑON ⎯5,000
SONORAN JUNIPER
SAGEBRUSH
LOWER ⎯3,000
SONORAN MESQUITE
AGAVE ⎯1,000
FEET

LIFE ZONES OF NATIVE VEGETATION

0   40   80

miles

4. LIFE ZONES OF NATIVE VEGETATION

THERE ARE SIX LIFE ZONES of native vegetation in New Mexico: Lower Sonoran, Upper Sonoran, Transition, Canadian, Hudsonian, and Arctic-Alpine. The sequence is from warmest to coldest areas and from driest to wettest. Since altitude in New Mexico, more than latitude, accounts for climatic differences, the sequence is altitudinal, as it is in the tropics.

The "Lower Sonoran" is the zone of mesquite and black grama grass. It is found in the Río Grande Valley below Socorro, in the Pecos Valley up to Santa Rosa, and in most of the southwestern part of the state. Usually at altitudes below 4,500 feet, the grass coverage in this zone permits more grazing than is possible at higher elevations, thereby making it economically more valuable. It embraces an area of about 19,500 square miles.

The "Upper Sonoran" is a zone of blue grama and buffalo grass, the piñon, and juniper. Most of the plains, foothills, and valleys lying above 4,500 feet are included in this zone. It covers about three-fourths of the area of the entire state. Because the region is so vast, there is considerable variation in the vegetation. At the lower altitudes within this zone, vegetation is very scanty, the result of arid conditions. At the higher altitudes of the Upper Sonoran zone (8,000 to 8,500 feet) better stands of grass, sagebrush, piñon, and juniper show the obvious effect of more rainfall.

The "Transition" zone covers about 19,000 square miles and is identified with the ponderosa pine. It is found on the middle mountain slopes of the high ranges at altitudes of 7,000 to 8,500 feet on the northeast slopes, and 8,000 to 9,500 feet on the southwest slopes.

The "Canadian" is the zone of blue spruce and Douglas fir. Embracing about 4,000 square miles, and located between 8,500 and 9,500 feet, it is the most humid area of the state, and its rain- and snowfall feed the streams that irrigate the more arid regions. There is also some lumbering in this region.

The "Hudsonian" is a zone of dwarf spruce. It occurs in a narrow scrubby timberline belt around the higher peaks, above 9,500 feet. It covers only 160 square miles in New Mexico, and its only commercial use is summer pasture for sheep.

The "Arctic-Alpine" is the treeless zone of the low and hearty alpine plants identified with arctic tundra. It is found as a cap on the highest peaks and is important only because it frequently retains snow until late summer, when moisture is most needed in the dry valleys below.

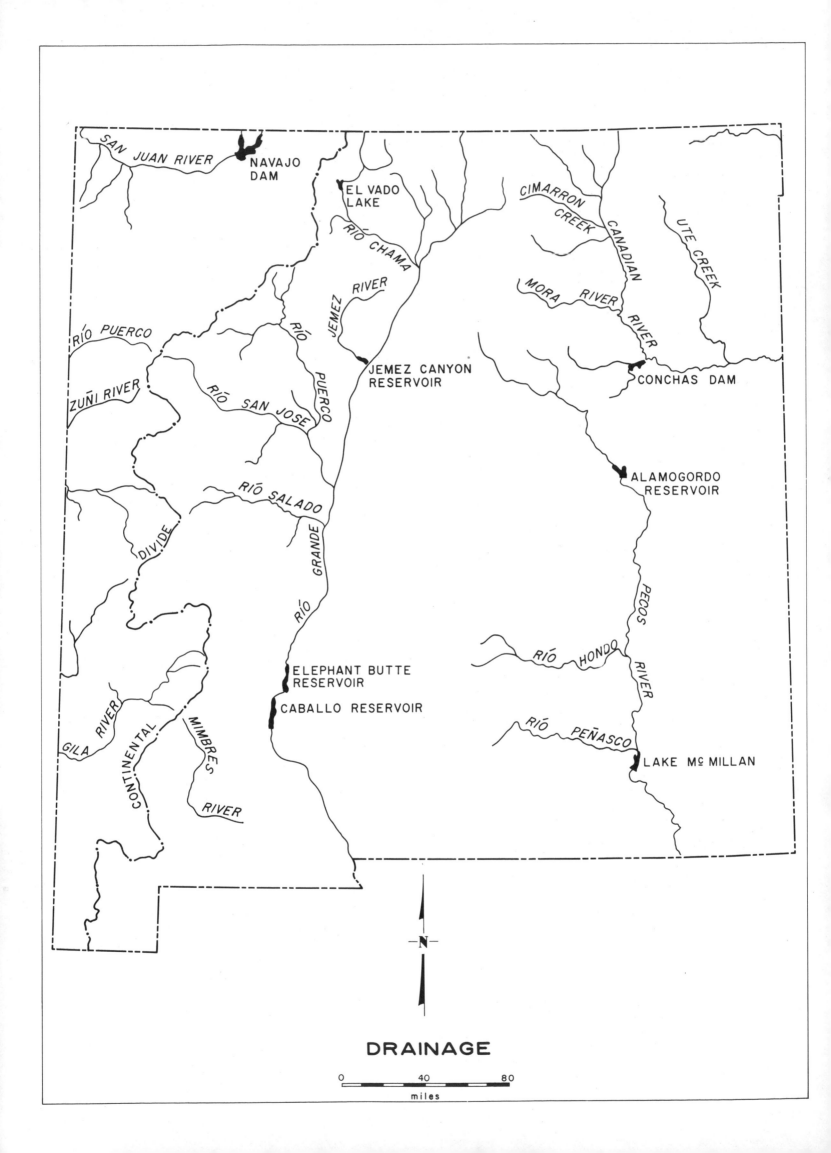

SAN JUAN RIVER

NAVAJO DAM

EL VADO LAKE

RÍO CHAMA

JEMEZ RIVER

CIMARRON CREEK

CANADIAN RIVER

UTE CREEK

RÍO PUERCO

MORA RIVER

ZUÑI RIVER

RÍO PUERCO

RÍO SAN JOSE

JEMEZ CANYON RESERVOIR

CONCHAS DAM

RÍO SALADO

ALAMOGORDO RESERVOIR

DIVIDE

RÍO GRANDE

PECOS RIVER

GILA RIVER

CONTINENTAL

MIMBRES RIVER

RÍO HONDO

ELEPHANT BUTTE RESERVOIR

CABALLO RESERVOIR

RÍO PEÑASCO

LAKE McMILLAN

N

DRAINAGE

0   40   80
miles

5. DRAINAGE

NEW MEXICO IS DRAINED by five major rivers—the Río Grande, Pecos, Canadian, San Juan, and Gila—and their tributaries. The only other noteworthy rivers are the Río Puerco and the Zuñi. Most of the state lies to the east of the continental divide.

The Río Grande, 1,800 miles in length, is one of the great rivers of the world; and because it virtually dissects the state, it has played a most influential role in New Mexico's history. The alluvial plain that has made possible man's agricultural use of the river ranges in width from a few feet in the northern part of the state to 1 to 5 miles on either side of the river in the southern part. Ruins of ancient villages and canals indicate that man probably practiced irrigation here more than a thousand years ago. Throughout the Spanish and Mexican eras, his use of New Mexico was limited to the Río Grande and the valleys of its tributaries. Agriculture in the valley remains an important industry to the present time. Unfortunately, frequent floods have limited productivity. Elephant Butte Reservoir and Caballo Reservoir, along with other installations upstream, have in recent years lessened damage caused by floods.

The Pecos River lies east of the Río Grande and follows a course approximately parallel to it. It was a popular route for explorers. Its flood-plain valley is highly productive when irrigated; but, unlike the Río Grande, it does not have a long record of use by man. A series of canals and dams was first built in 1888 near Carlsbad, and since that time reservoirs have held sufficient water to make many parts of its valley productive.

The Canadian River rises on the eastern slopes of the Sangre de Cristo Mountains and flows almost due east. It was a useful avenue for American explorers, who entered New Mexico in spite of the fact that the river had cut a deep trough in the High Plains, in some places 1,000 feet deep. Although there were a few primitive attempts at agriculture, it was not until 1940 that Conchas Dam impounded sufficient water to permit extensive irrigation farming near Tucumcari.

The San Juan River flows southwest from Colorado. Thirty miles from where the stream enters New Mexico, its course changes westward for 124 miles before leaving the state. The valley formed by the San Juan is 1 to 4 miles wide and has fertile river-bottom lands along its course. The recently completed Navajo Dam has made it possible to convert the surrounding valleys into fertile farmland. Unlike the Pecos and the Canadian, the San Juan was probably the site of prominent Indian civilizations before the coming of the white man.

The Gila River rises in the high Mogollon and Black Range Mountains of southwestern New Mexico. It flows southwesterly across Grant and Hidalgo counties, draining 6,100 square miles before reaching the Arizona line. Because the river flows through a narrow canyon for much of its course, irrigation has been limited. The frequent floods which plague the Gila have earned it the reputation of being "the world's muddiest river." Like the San Juan, it too was the site of Indian civilizations before the coming of the white man. The Gila was originally a boundary line between Mexico and the United States, after the Cession of 1848.

All of the large lakes in New Mexico are man-made. They have been built for such purposes as flood control, conservation, irrigation, recreation, power, and municipal water supply.

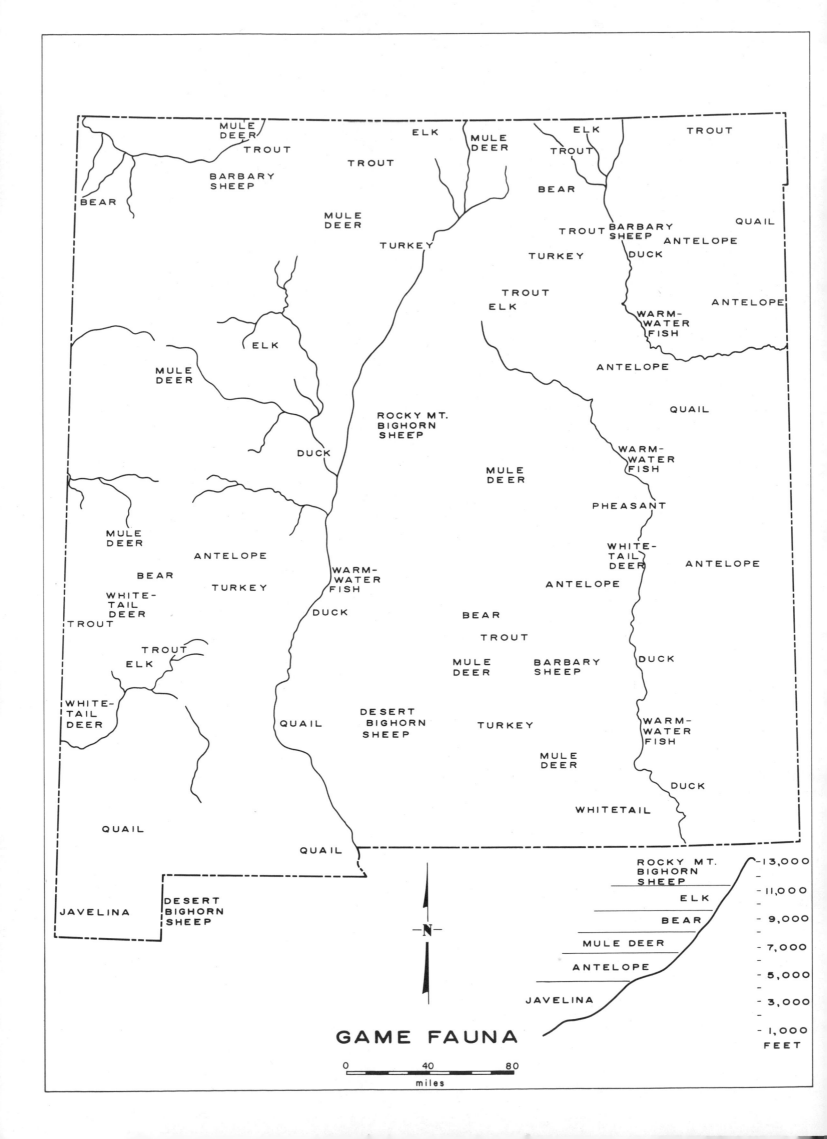

MULE DEER
TROUT
BARBARY SHEEP
BEAR
ELK
TROUT
MULE DEER
ELK
TROUT
TROUT
MULE DEER
TURKEY
BEAR
QUAIL
TROUT
BARBARY SHEEP
ANTELOPE
TURKEY
DUCK
ANTELOPE
MULE DEER
TROUT
ELK
WARM-WATER FISH
ELK
MULE DEER
ANTELOPE
ROCKY MT. BIGHORN SHEEP
QUAIL
DUCK
WARM-WATER FISH
MULE DEER
MULE DEER
PHEASANT
ANTELOPE
BEAR
WHITE-TAIL DEER
WHITE-TAIL DEER
TROUT
ANTELOPE
ANTELOPE
TURKEY
WARM-WATER FISH
TROUT
ELK
DUCK
BEAR
TROUT
WHITE-TAIL DEER
MULE DEER
BARBARY SHEEP
DUCK
QUAIL
DESERT BIGHORN SHEEP
TURKEY
WARM-WATER FISH
MULE DEER
QUAIL
DUCK
QUAIL
WHITETAIL
JAVELINA
DESERT BIGHORN SHEEP

ROCKY MT. BIGHORN SHEEP ─ 13,000
─ 11,000
ELK
─ 9,000
BEAR
MULE DEER ─ 7,000
─ 5,000
ANTELOPE
─ 3,000
JAVELINA
─ 1,000
FEET

N

GAME FAUNA

0   40   80
miles

6. GAME FAUNA

ONE OF THE MOST ATTRACTIVE FEATURES of New Mexico has been its great variety of animals and birds. Castañeda, the chronicler of the Coronado expedition in 1540, reported seeing "cows covered with frizzled hair (buffalo) which resembles wool," and "a great many native fowl in these provinces, and cocks (wild turkeys) with great hanging chins." Sportsmen ever since then have hunted and fished throughout the state. Unfortunately, game laws were at first slow to be enforced, and game fauna —such as elk, deer, antelope, and turkeys—all but disappeared.

The diversity of natural vegetation zones, the inaccessibility of many areas, and the evolution of an effective game policy have reversed the trend. Some success has even been attained in reintroducing elk and many species of game birds into the state.

Being a part of the so-called African Strip which stretches from West Texas to California, New Mexico has participated in the effort to bring in game animals from similar geographic areas of the world. This revolutionary plan of importation was inaug-

urated by the game commissioners of New Mexico in the early 1950's. First introduced were Barbary sheep from North Africa. Their ability to adapt and prosper in the rugged terrain of the Canadian River country has led to extensive plans to bring other game animals to the Southwest from Asia, Africa, and even Europe. Not only would such a program create better and more varied hunting; it would also save these species from possible extinction in their native habitat.

Approximately three hundred different species of birds can be found in New Mexico at almost any time of the year. Their distribution, like that of all wildlife in the state, is mainly determined by altitude. Their importance in control of insects harmful to farm produce has been recognized, and efforts have been made to improve the natural habitat of birds other than the game variety. As the number of predatory animals has decreased, the number of birds, as well as other types of wildlife, has increased.

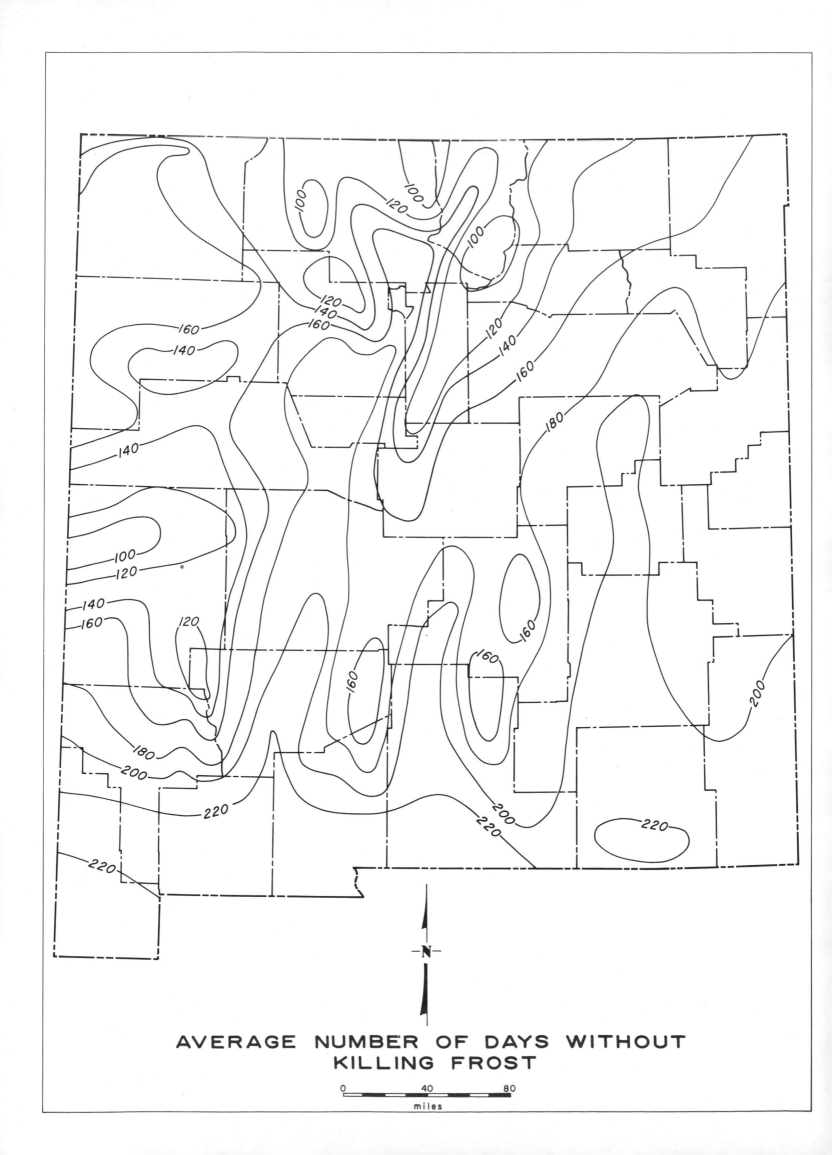

AVERAGE NUMBER OF DAYS WITHOUT KILLING FROST

-N-

0   40   80
miles

7. AVERAGE NUMBER OF DAYS WITHOUT KILLING FROST

THE AVERAGE DATES of killing frost set the period of safe plant growth and are thus a decisive factor in choosing the kinds of crops to plant and the sequence in which to plant them in a given area. In general, the growing season (i.e., the frost-free period) ranges from 148 to 220 days. The variation is, naturally, caused by latitude and altitude. Fortunately, the longer growing season is normally found in areas under irrigation, while shorter seasons occur where they can influence only the grassland. The maximum average number of days without killing frost is found in the Deming-Lordsburg area of southwestern New Mexico, along the lower end of the Río Grande Valley, and in a small area in the Pecos River valley south of Carlsbad. The minimum average number of days without killing frost is 100 around Taos, Tres Piedras, and Gavilan.

New Mexico is characterized by diversity. The mean annual temperature of the state is about 53° F. and varies as much as 26° at different stations. The variations are caused more by altitude than latitude. The temperature variation northward is 1.5° to 2.5° F. for every degree of latitude. However, for every 1,000 feet of elevation, the temperature gradient is 5° F. This effect of altitude upon temperature is readily noted by comparing the July average of Santa Fe (elevation 6,696 feet), which is 69.2°, with that of Santa Rosa (elevation 4,616 feet), 77.5°. Deming (elevation 4,331 feet) records a July average of 80.2°, whereas Silver City (elevation 5,595 feet), only a short distance away, has an average of 74.9° for the same month.

Statistics, of course, fail to tell the full story of climate. Washington, D.C., on a hot muggy day, where the temperature reaches only 90° F., but then falls to only 75° at night, may be far less comfortable for human habitation than Carlsbad, where the temperature may soar to 100° during the day, but then may fall to 65° at night. In this instance, the statistical average might be the same, but the sensible temperature (that temperature which people feel) may be quite different. One of the prime determinants of the sensible temperature is the amount of moisture in the air. Evaporation involves taking much sensible heat from the body surface, and cooling results; the more evaporation, the more the body will cool. When the air is hot and damp, there can be little evaporation and thus little cooling of the body. Consequently, the air becomes oppressive to human beings. So "dry" heat can be tolerated with much less discomfort than heat when the air is moist. New Mexico, having the lowest average humidity of any state, has a pleasant "sensible" temperature.

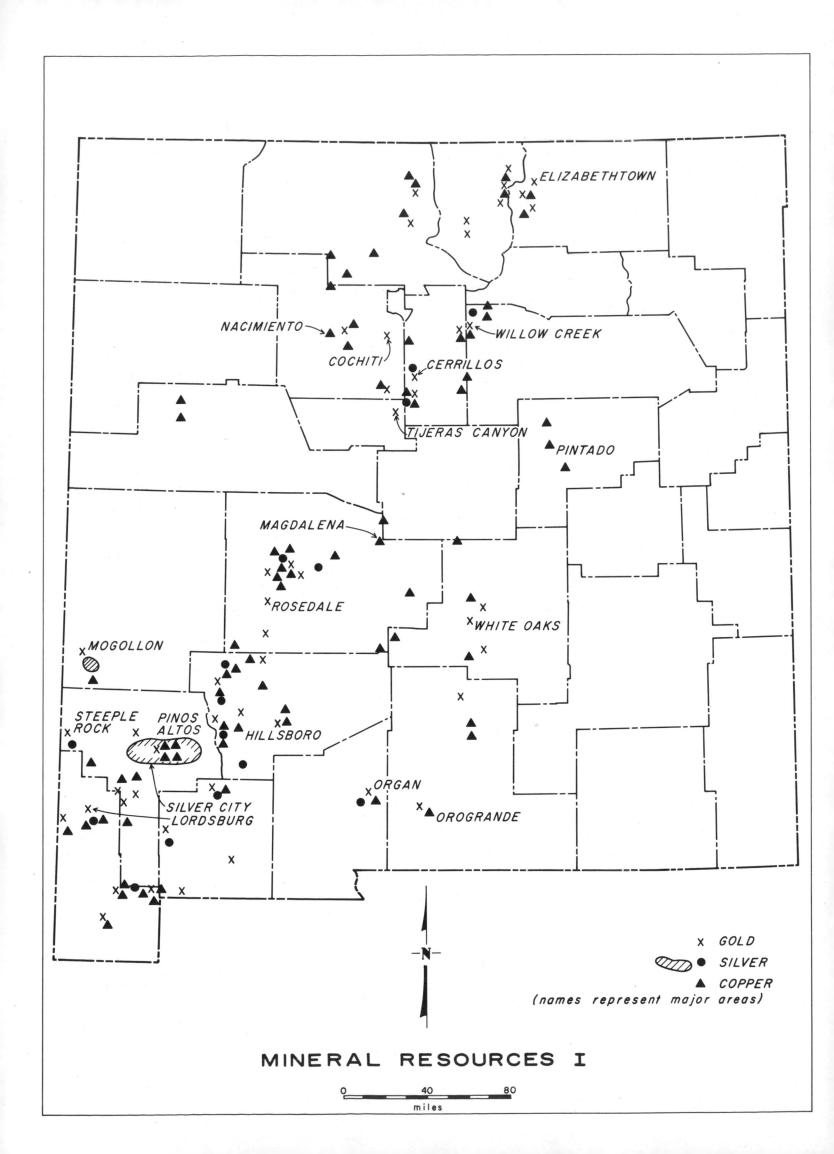

NACIMIENTO
COCHITI
CERRILLOS
WILLOW CREEK
ELIZABETHTOWN
TIJERAS CANYON
PINTADO
MAGDALENA
ROSEDALE
WHITE OAKS
MOGOLLON
STEEPLE
ROCK
PINOS
ALTOS
HILLSBORO
SILVER CITY
LORDSBURG
ORGAN
OROGRANDE

X GOLD
SILVER
COPPER
(names represent major areas)

-N-

MINERAL RESOURCES I

0   40   80
miles

8. MINERAL RESOURCES—I & II

EXPLOITATION OF MINERAL RESOURCES has always played a key role in the history of New Mexico. In fact, the Spanish gave this remote province its name hoping that it would produce mineral wealth equivalent to that of Mexico. Cabeza de Vaca in 1535 reported seeing within the state "many signs of gold, antimony, iron, copper, and other metals." Fray Marcos de Niza reported that this was "a land rich in gold, silver, and other wealth." Hope of finding precious metals such as these motivated the Coronado expedition, as well as the conquest of Don Juan de Oñate.

There was undoubtedly some mining in the eighteenth century, but actual mineral exploitation began in 1804 in the copper deposits of Santa Rita in the southwestern part of the state. Santa Rita remained active in the Mexican era, but was not worked extensively until the Apaches were subdued in the 1870's and the railroads arrived in the 1880's. Although it lacks the glamour of gold and silver, mined copper has been of much greater value than the other two. As the map indicates, copper is found in many different areas of the state, but 90 per cent of the state's production still comes from Grant County.

Gold mining began in 1828 in the Ortiz Mountains between Albuquerque and Santa Fe and continued through the rest of the Mexican period. In the post–Civil War period a series of gold mining "booms" occurred in various parts of the state, especially Elizabethtown. Much gold was mined in the nineteenth century, but there has been a steady decline in recent years, so much so that the industry is no longer prominent. Because of lack of water for mining, gold mining in New Mexico awaits the perfection of a dry extraction method.

Silver mining has been confined mainly to the southwestern portion of the state. Like gold mining, it began to decline in importance in 1905, and today production is negligible.

Lead and zinc are usually found in the same areas as copper and are also mined mainly in the southwestern part of the state. Their peak year was 1952, when total production was valued at $19,185,000. Since that year the value has declined. Iron ore is found in limited quantities within the state but has never been of significant value.

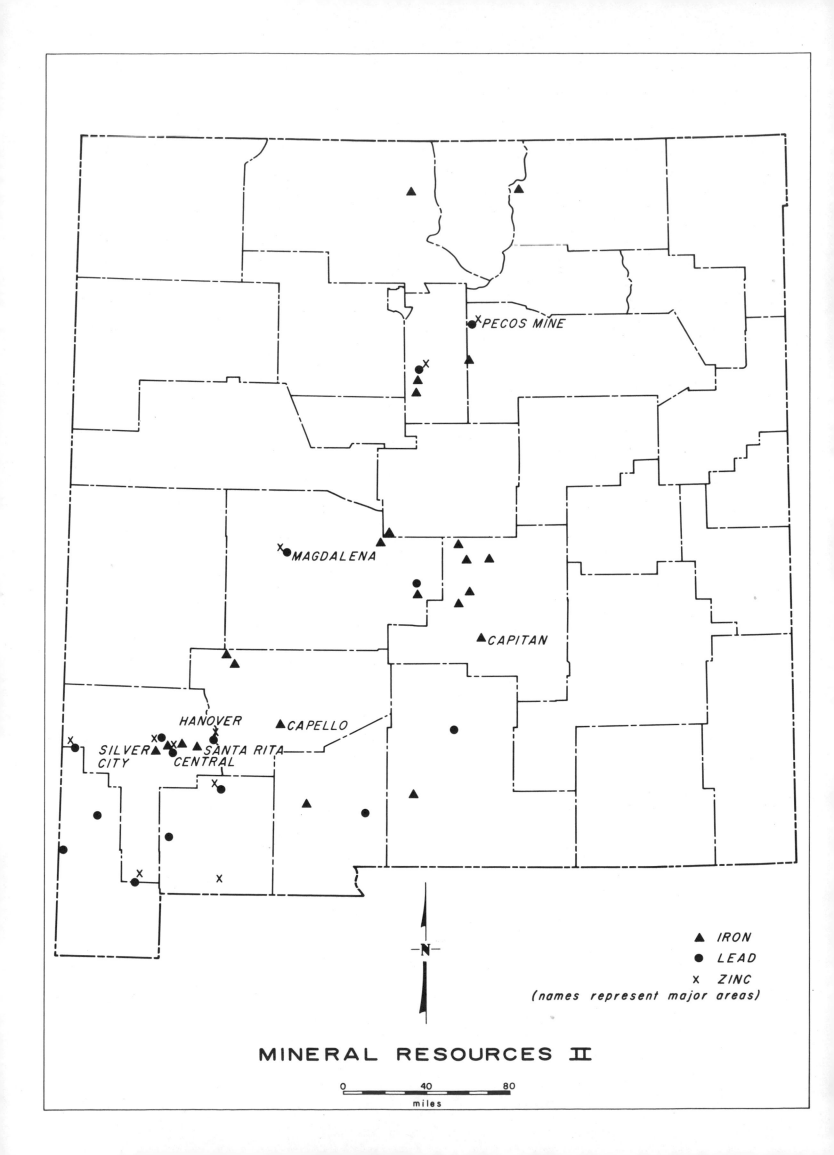

PECOS MINE

MAGDALENA

CAPITAN

HANOVER

CAPELLO

SILVER
CITY

SANTA RITA

CENTRAL

N

▲ IRON

● LEAD

✕ ZINC

(names represent major areas)

MINERAL RESOURCES II

0   40   80
miles

8. MINERAL RESOURCES—II

(A description of this map is included in the discussion on the preceding page.)

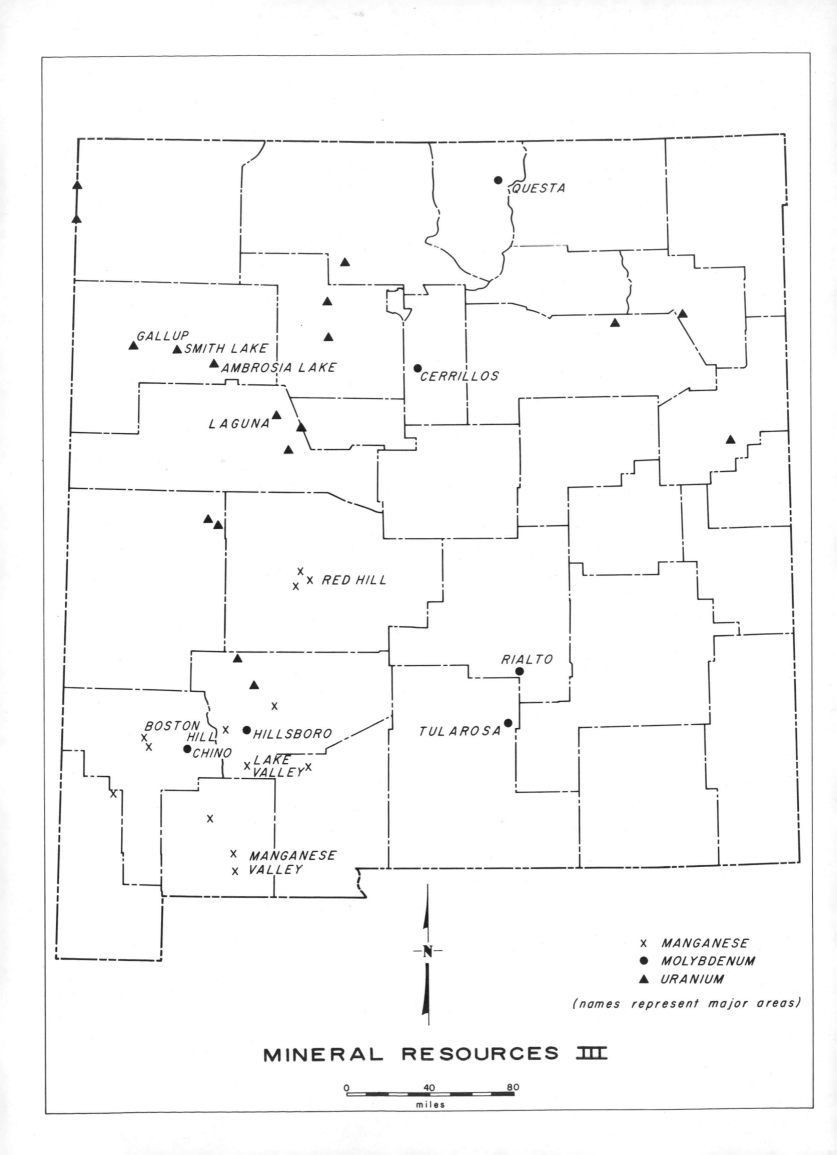

●QUESTA

GALLUP
▲ SMITH LAKE
▲ AMBROSIA LAKE

●CERRILLOS

LAGUNA ▲

X
X X RED HILL
X

RIALTO ●

X

BOSTON
HILL X ● HILLSBORO
X CHINO
X X ● LAKE
X VALLEY X

TULAROSA ●

X

X MANGANESE
X VALLEY

─ N ─

X MANGANESE
● MOLYBDENUM
▲ URANIUM

(names represent major areas)

MINERAL RESOURCES III

0   40   80
miles

9. MINERAL RESOURCES—III & IV

THE NEWEST ADDITION to the New Mexico family of minerals is uranium. Its value was unknown only a few years ago, but today is very high. Uranium was accidently discovered by a Navaho in the spring of 1950 near Grants, and production is concentrated in this area, although there are widely scattered deposits throughout the state. New Mexico led the nation in production in 1964.

Demand for manganese, the ferroalloy so valuable in steelmaking, has increased since World War II, because the Cold War has interfered with overseas sources.

Molybdenum, another ferroalloy, has also become more valuable in recent years. The richest deposits are found near Questa in the Red River area. In the past, most of molybdenum was mined in mineral-rich Grant County as a by-product of copper, and in scattered areas of the state.

The real giant of the New Mexico mineral industry is petroleum. Today it brings in more than one-half the revenue of all the state's mineral production. The original drilling area was the Permian Basin in the southeastern corner of the state. Since World War II the San Juan Basin in the northwestern corner has also become an important source of petroleum.

Natural gas is another valuable mineral resource. In the Permian Basin it is found as a by-product of petroleum, but the field in the San Juan Basin has distinct gas wells extracting dry gas. As has been true of petroleum, natural gas can be carried by pipelines to population centers. Helium gas is produced at Des Moines and Bueyeros, and in the Estancia Valley.

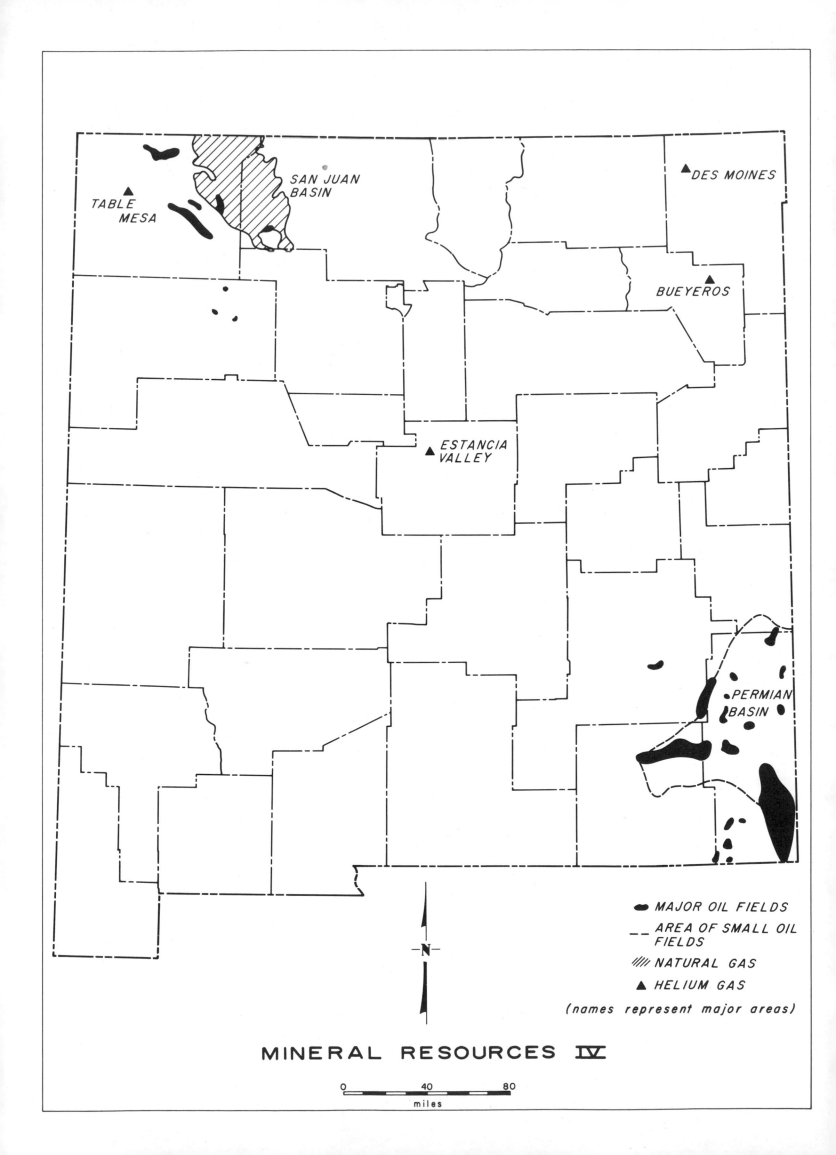

TABLE
MESA ▲

SAN JUAN
BASIN

▲ DES MOINES

BUEYEROS ▲

ESTANCIA
VALLEY ▲

PERMIAN
BASIN

🮲 MAJOR OIL FIELDS

‒ ‒ AREA OF SMALL OIL
FIELDS

//// NATURAL GAS

▲ HELIUM GAS

(names represent major areas)

N

MINERAL RESOURCES Ⅳ

0   40   80
miles

9. MINERAL RESOURCES—IV

(A description of this map is included in the discussion on the preceding page.)

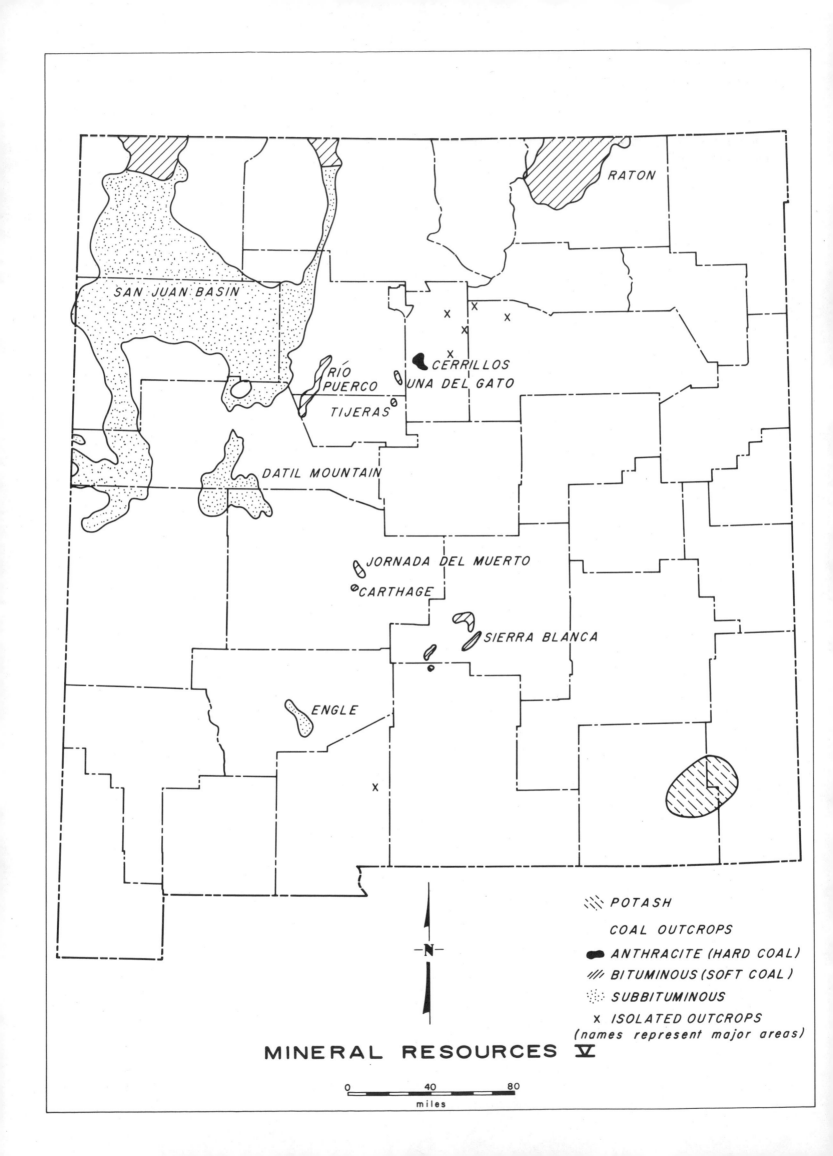

RATON

SAN JUAN BASIN

X   X
    X
    X
CERRILLOS
UNA DEL GATO
RÍO
PUERCO
TIJERAS

DATIL MOUNTAIN

JORNADA DEL MUERTO
CARTHAGE

SIERRA BLANCA

ENGLE

X

N

POTASH

COAL OUTCROPS

ANTHRACITE (HARD COAL)

BITUMINOUS (SOFT COAL)

SUBBITUMINOUS

X ISOLATED OUTCROPS
(names represent major areas)

MINERAL RESOURCES V

0   40   80
miles

COAL MINING IN NEW MEXICO has been vital during the past century. In a state where many regions are short of wood for fuel, it can be assumed that coal was used, but records have not been kept of the usage of so common an item. The army used coal during the Civil War, and even Texas ranchers were forced to bring in wagonloads of coal for fuel.

The coming of the railroads between 1879 and 1882 put coal production on a firm footing. The first area opened was in Colfax County near Raton, and this district traditionally led the state in production. In 1882 the railroad reached Gallup, and existing mines in the neighborhood were promptly put into production to supply most of the coal used by locomotives en route to California.

When coal mining was at its peak, the Raton field and the portion of the San Juan Basin near Gallup accounted for about 90 per cent of the state's total coal output, although mines throughout the state were worked to supply local needs. For example, mines in Lincoln County employed 300 men to produce over 120,000 tons of coal in 1902.

At its top production in 1918 the coal industry in New Mexico produced more than 4,000,000 tons of coal per year from sixty-one mines and employed 5,000 workers. But the dieselization of the railroads and use of oil and gas for heating led to a steady decline of the coal industry in New Mexico. This downturn, however, has been reversed in recent years, and in 1964 total production was at 94 per cent of the 1918 level. Most of the coal mined has been bituminous or subbituminous, although some anthracite has come from the Cerrillos field near Madrid.

Production of potash in New Mexico is of comparatively recent origin and is a growing mining activity instead of a declining one. At times the rate of growth has been nothing short of spectacular. Since approximately 85 per cent of the nation's potash comes from a small area near Carlsbad, its contribution to the state's economy is large. Potash is used mainly for commercial fertilizers, and until World War I the American supply came from Germany. Because of the shortage created by the war, the United States Geological Survey searched for a domestic supply. In 1925 an oil geologist accidentally discovered the deposits near Carlsbad. These deposits lie in horizontal beds 4 to 10 feet thick at a depth below the surface varying from 500 to 3,800 feet. Potash lies in seams, and is mined in much the same way as coal.

Scattered throughout New Mexico are many deposits of minerals that have been barely touched, if at all. They do, however, have a potential for future exploitation.

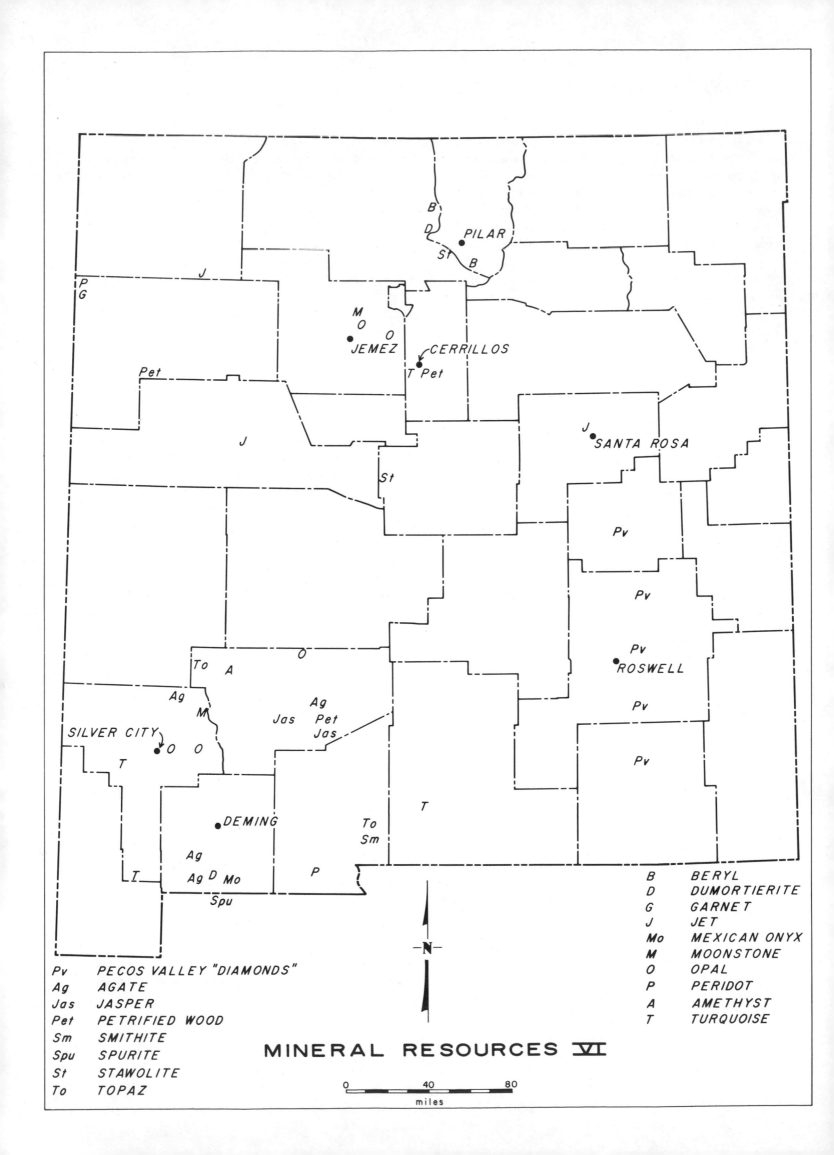

B • PILAR
D
St B
J
P
G
M O O
• JEMEZ CERRILLOS
Pet T Pet

J
• SANTA ROSA

Pet

St

Pv

J

Pv

O
To A
Ag Pv
M • ROSWELL
SILVER CITY Jas Ag Pv
T O O Pet
Jas

Pv

T

To
Sm

Ag
Ag D Mo P
Spu

N

MINERAL RESOURCES VI

Pv   PECOS VALLEY "DIAMONDS"   B   BERYL
Ag   AGATE   D   DUMORTIERITE
Jas   JASPER   G   GARNET
Pet   PETRIFIED WOOD   J   JET
Sm   SMITHITE   Mo   MEXICAN ONYX
Spu   SPURITE   M   MOONSTONE
St   STAWOLITE   O   OPAL
To   TOPAZ   P   PERIDOT
                                      A   AMETHYST
                                      T   TURQUOISE

DEMING •

0   40   80
miles

10. MINERAL RESOURCES—VI

(A description of this map is included in the discussion on the preceding page.)

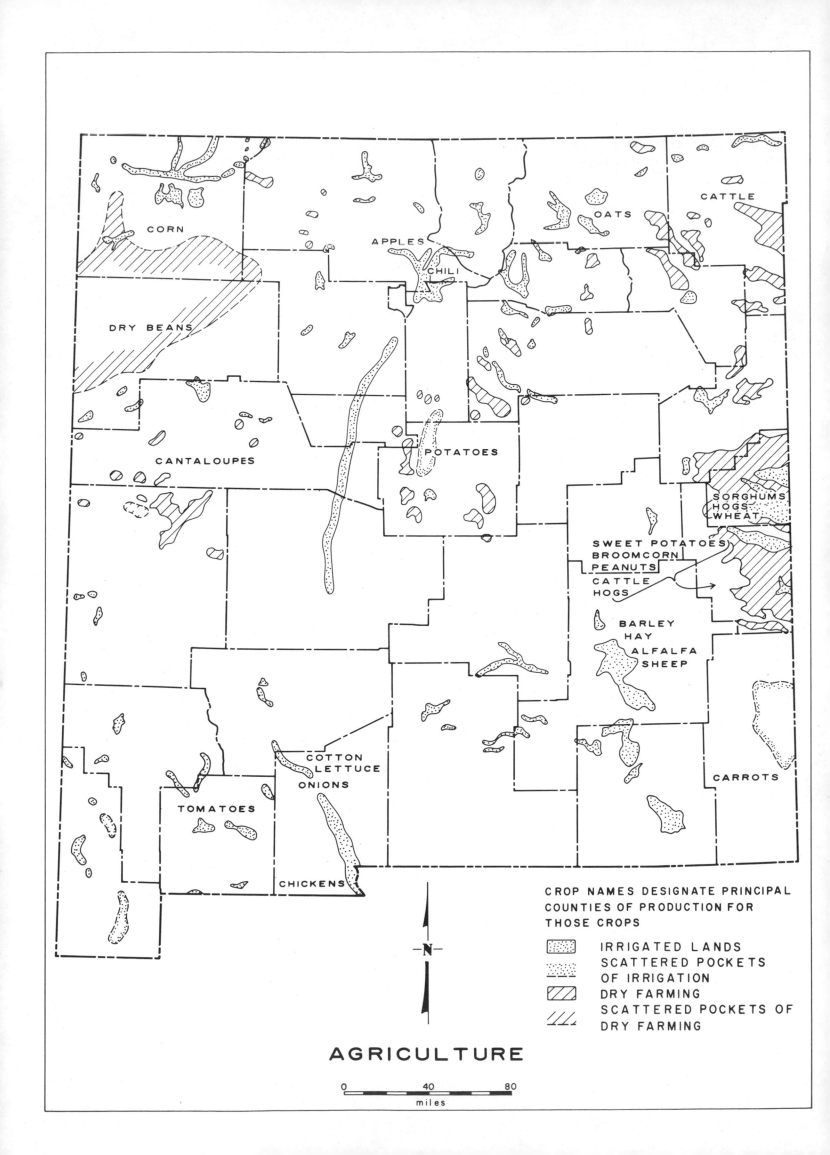

CORN

CATTLE

OATS

APPLES

CHILI

DRY BEANS

CANTALOUPES

POTATOES

SORGHUMS
HOGS
WHEAT

SWEET POTATOES
BROOMCORN
PEANUTS
CATTLE
HOGS

BARLEY
HAY
ALFALFA
SHEEP

CARROTS

COTTON
LETTUCE
ONIONS

TOMATOES

CHICKENS

N

CROP NAMES DESIGNATE PRINCIPAL
COUNTIES OF PRODUCTION FOR
THOSE CROPS

IRRIGATED LANDS
SCATTERED POCKETS
OF IRRIGATION
DRY FARMING
SCATTERED POCKETS OF
DRY FARMING

AGRICULTURE

0   40   80
miles

11. AGRICULTURE

INHABITANTS OF NEW MEXICO have tilled the soil for many centuries. Long before the white man came, the sedentary Indians of the state based their civilization on corn and even used irrigation. Floodwater farming, however, was practiced more than irrigation. By this method, crops were planted in the fields of alluvial soil once the water had subsided. Plants such as beans, corn, cotton, and squash were the main items raised this way. Floodwater farming was done not only by the prehistoric settlers but also by the Mexicans when they first arrived in the area. It survives into the present in isolated areas of New Mexico and is relatively common in portions of South America.

Sheep raising was the primary agrarian pursuit under Spain and Mexico, the raising of cattle becoming important in the post–Civil War era. Livestock marketing has retained its position in the state, but since the coming of the railroads in 1879, emphasis on agriculture has increased. Anglo settlers first made the mistake of trying to raise crops suited to more humid climates, to their sorrow. In the twentieth century a system of dry farming has developed which stresses the growing of wheat and many varieties of the grain sorghums.

One-half of the total cropland of 1,135,000 acres is under either surface- or ground-water irrigation, and it is from such lands that the overwhelming share of the crop dollar comes. Cotton remains the leading cash crop and is second only to cattle in terms of marketing receipts. Hay, wheat, and peanuts are the other significant crops.

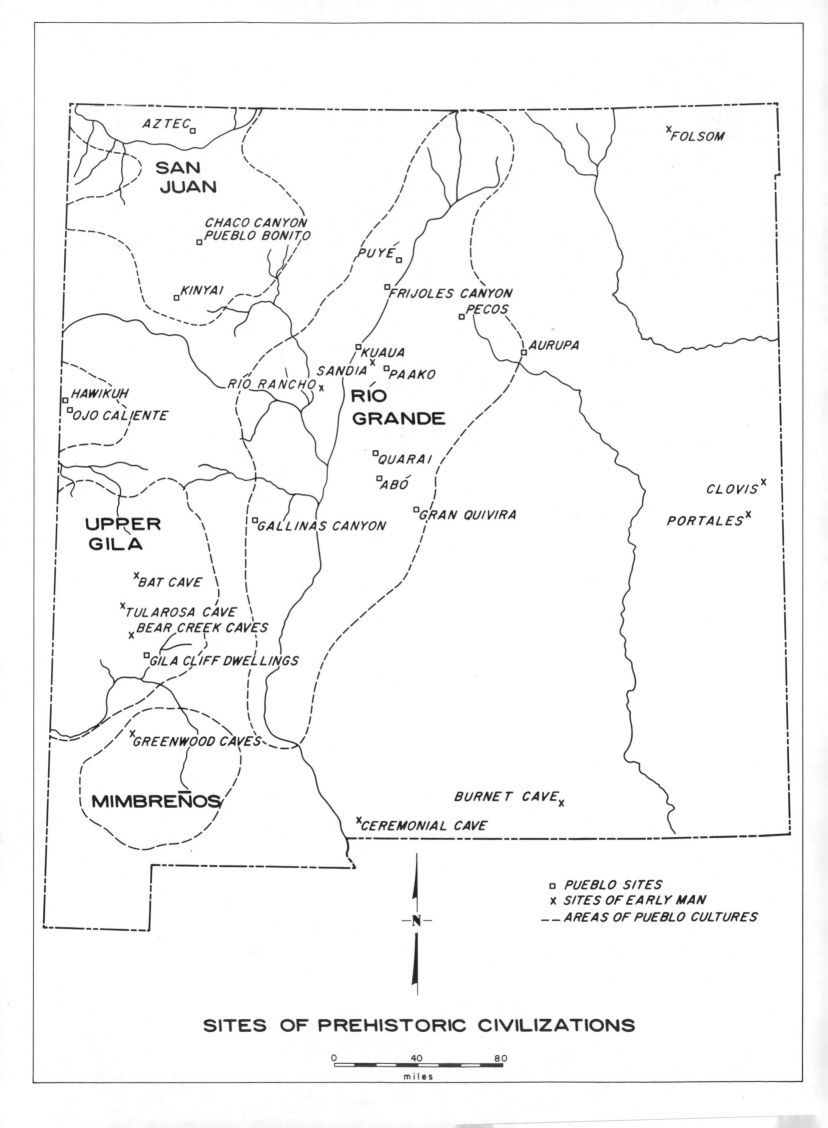

AZTEC

SAN JUAN

×FOLSOM

CHACO CANYON
PUEBLO BONITO

PUYÉ

KINYAI

FRIJOLES CANYON
PECOS

KUAUA
SANDIA ×
×PAAKO

AURUPA

HAWIKUH
OJO CALIENTE

RIO RANCHO ×

RÍO
GRANDE

QUARAI

ABÓ

CLOVIS ×

UPPER
GILA

GALLINAS CANYON

GRAN QUIVIRA

PORTALES ×

×BAT CAVE

×TULAROSA CAVE
BEAR CREEK CAVES
×

GILA CLIFF DWELLINGS

×GREENWOOD CAVES

MIMBREÑOS

BURNET CAVE ×

×CEREMONIAL CAVE

□ PUEBLO SITES
× SITES OF EARLY MAN
-- AREAS OF PUEBLO CULTURES

—N—

SITES OF PREHISTORIC CIVILIZATIONS

0   40   80
miles

12. SITES OF PREHISTORIC CIVILIZATIONS

SINCE THE SPANIARDS FIRST ARRIVED in New Mexico, evidences of very early civilizations have been discovered. The earliest culture known is that of Sandia Man, named after the cave in which artifacts dating back 25,000 years have been found. More famous is Folsom Man, named after the town near which man-made objects of this early civilization were found. Projectile points of Folsom Man have been uncovered throughout the Southwest, and indicate that these people lived in the area 10,000 to 25,000 years ago. Leading sites of such discoveries are Blackwater Draw near Portales, and Burnet Cave in the Guadalupe Mountains. Various other signs constantly being uncovered prove the presence of early man within the state at different periods in the past.

The Anasazi culture was centered in the San Juan Basin, and possibly reached as far south as Zuñi. These people were probably the ancestors of most of the latter-day Pueblo Indians and undoubtedly influenced other cultures greatly. They were superior to other Indians in construction of large multistoried buildings and in the quality of the baskets they wove. The Mogollon culture existed in the Upper Gila area from 300 B.C. to A.D. 1100. The Mogollones were also an agricultural people, who lived in pit houses and cliff houses. The Mimbreño culture, probably a later stage of the Mogollon civilization, was characterized by more Pueblo influence.

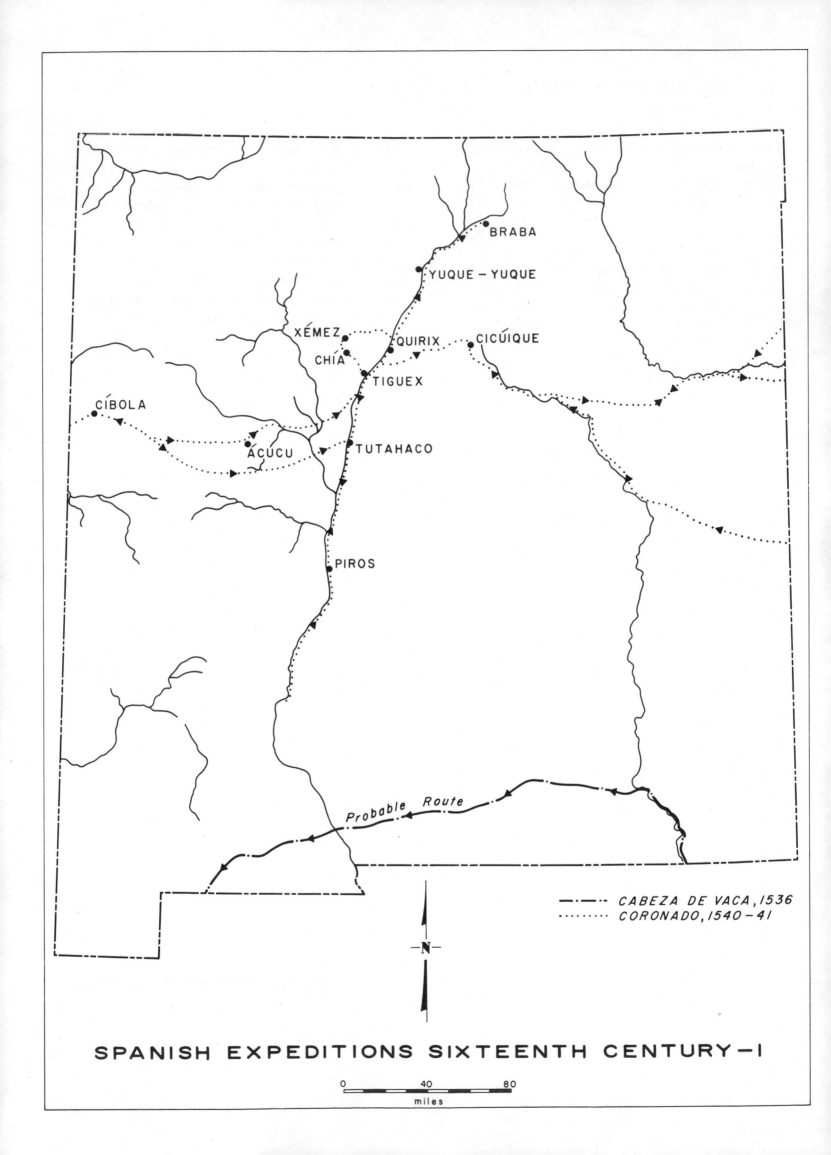

BRABA

YUQUE – YUQUE

XÉMEZ

QUIRIX   CICÚIQUE

CHIA

TIGUEX

CÍBOLA

ACUCU   TUTAHACO

PIROS

Probable   Route

—N—

CABEZA DE VACA, 1536
CORONADO, 1540-41

SPANISH EXPEDITIONS SIXTEENTH CENTURY–I

0   40   80

miles

13. SPANISH EXPEDITIONS: SIXTEENTH CENTURY—I

THE FIRST AUTHENTIC INFORMATION about New Mexico was brought to the Spaniards as a by-product of their attempt to settle Florida in 1528. Sailing back to Mexico, the survivors were shipwrecked near the present site of Galveston. Of the estimated total of 250, only 4 survived: Cabeza de Vaca, Dorantes, Castillo, and Esteban, a Moorish slave of Dorantes. Held captive by the Indians for a time, they were able to escape in 1534. Making their way across Texas, they ascended the Pecos for some distance, and then, striking westward, crossed the Río Grande some distance above the present site of El Paso. The stories Cabeza de Vaca and his companions told about the large settlements of Indians who possessed great quantities of precious metals led to subsequent Spanish explorations.

The initial exploration in New Mexico was headed by Francisco Vásquez de Coronado in 1540–41. The expedition was sponsored by Viceroy Antonio de Mendoza of Mexico, who, in naming the area "New" Mexico, revealed his hope that this region would contain tremendous quantities of gold and silver, as had the land of the Aztecs. Entering New Mexico near the fabled "Seven Golden Cities of Cíbola," Coronado followed a route eastward approximating that of the present-day Highway 66. Although the initial disappointment to Coronado and his men in not finding wealthy Indians to conquer must have been great, they were not easily discouraged. Exploratory expeditions went out in various directions. One of these found the Grand Canyon in Arizona. Others found the Pueblo Indian villages along the Río Grande. One Coronado lieutenant made extensive explorations eastward across the Llano Estacado, and the main force went as far east as Lyons, Kansas, where they expected to find the heralded Indian city of Quivira. Because the expedition found no trace of precious metals, it was considered a failure.

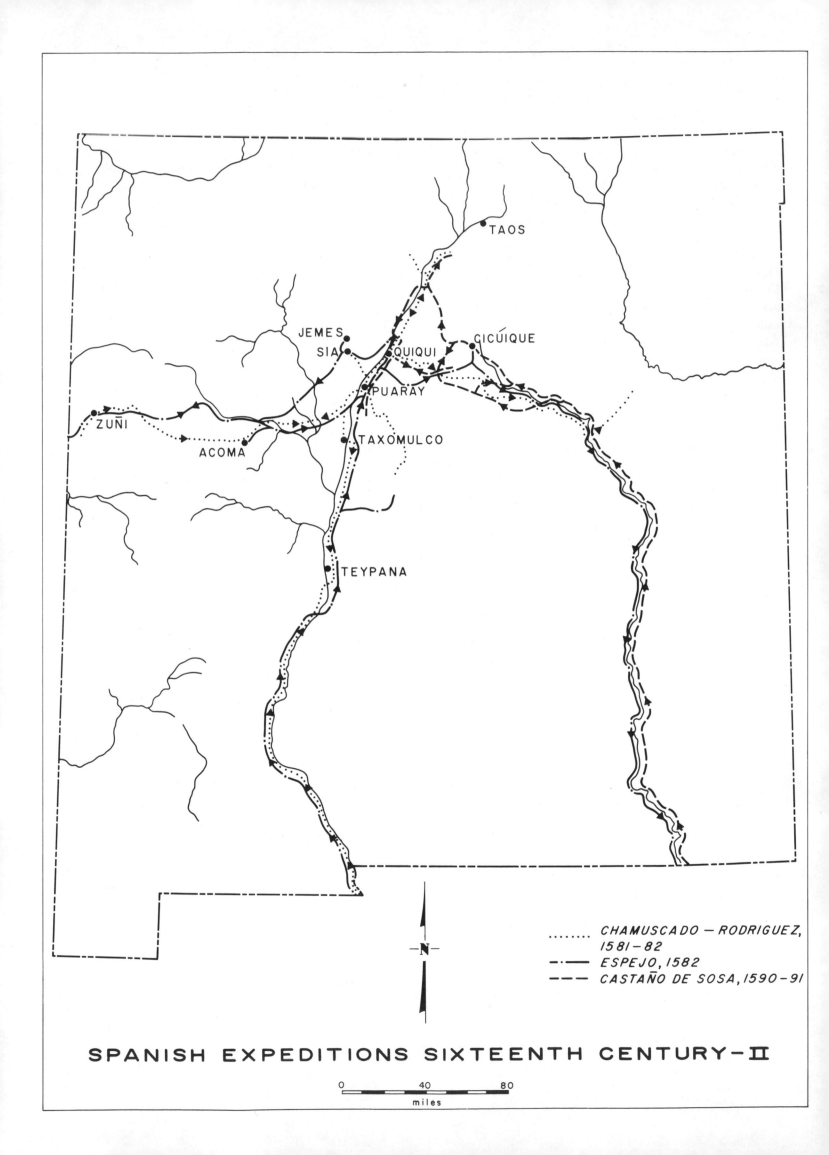

TAOS

JEMES
SIA
QUIQUI
CICÚIQUE

PUARAY

ZUÑI

ACOMA
TAXOMULCO

TEYPANA

N

.... CHAMUSCADO — RODRIGUEZ,
            1581–82
—·—·— ESPEJO, 1582
— — — CASTAÑO DE SOSA, 1590–91

SPANISH EXPEDITIONS SIXTEENTH CENTURY–II

0   40   80
miles

14. SPANISH EXPEDITIONS: SIXTEENTH CENTURY—II

FAILURE OF THE EXTENSIVE Coronado expeditions dashed hopes that another storehouse of treasure like that found in the Aztec Empire was available in New Mexico. The Mixtón War, which ravaged the frontier of New Spain, also curtailed exploration so that the natives along the Río Grande were left undisturbed for forty years. However, the Spanish mining frontier slowly edged northward, and prospectors, as well as slave hunters who fanned outward seeking unwilling Indian labor, heard stories of settled peoples far to the north.

One Agustín Rodríguez, a Franciscan lay brother, proposed a missionary expedition into the rumored area. The total party consisted of three friars, nine soldiers led by Francisco Sanchez Chamuscado, and nineteen Indians. Blazing a new route up the Río Grande in 1581, they visited most of the pueblo country. Two of the friars elected to remain behind when the main party returned to New Spain.

The Franciscan brethren of the two friars who had remained in New Mexico planned a relief party. Late in 1582, Antonio de Espejo, a wealthy rancher, outfitted such an expedition. Leading a small group up the Río Grande, where they learned of the martyrdom of the friars left behind, Espejo visited most of the pueblos, possibly went as far west as Prescott, Arizona, and then returned to New Spain via the Pecos River.

Reports of these expeditions led the Spanish Crown to plan permanent settlements in New Mexico. Before the authorities could act, Gaspar Castáño de Sosa, Lieutenant Governor and Captain General of Nuevo Leon, undertook a colonizing expedition in 1590–91. The group of 160 to 170 went up the Pecos River to the pueblo country. Although the purposes of the venture were not carried out, the expedition helped make possible the successful colonizing effort of Juan de Oñate in 1598.

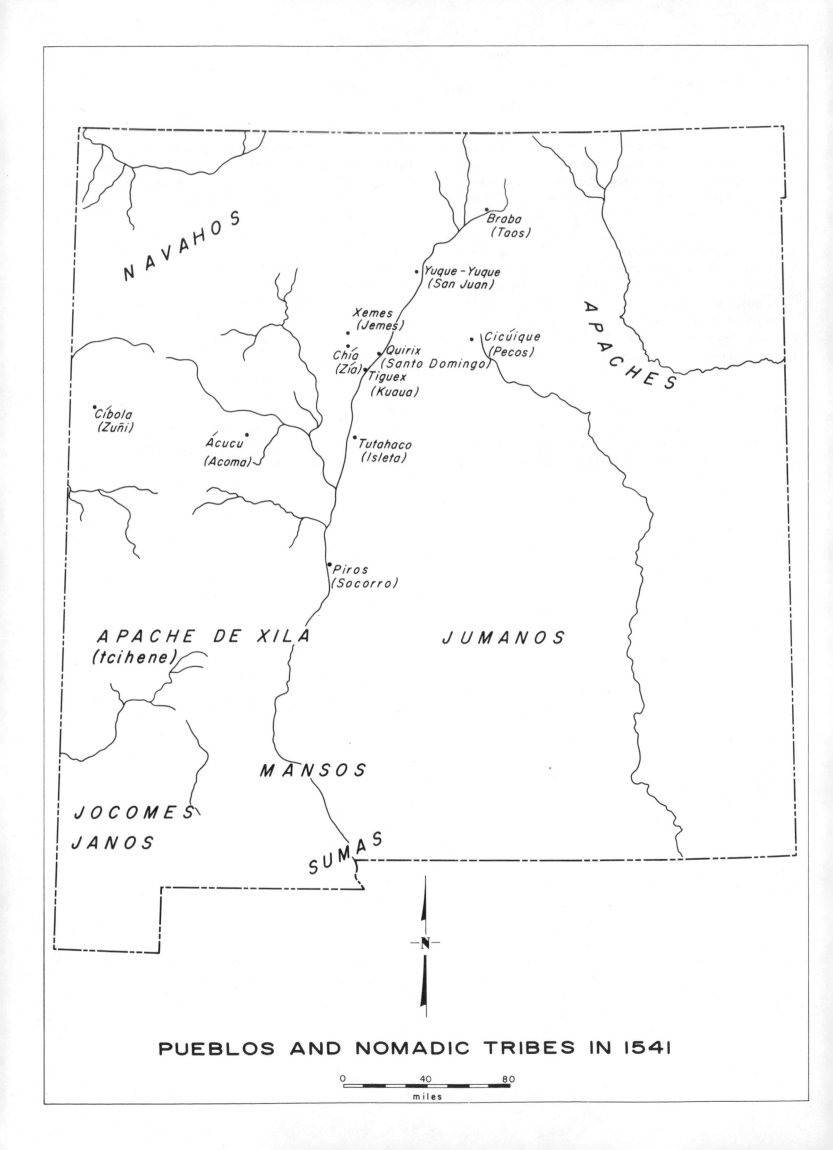

NAVAHOS

APACHES

• Braba
(Taos)

• Yuque - Yuque
(San Juan)

Xemes
(Jemes)
•

Chía
(Zía)
•

Quirix
(Santo Domingo)
•

• Cicúique
(Pecos)

Tiguex
(Kuaua)

• Cíbola
(Zuñi)

Ácucu
(Acoma)
•

• Tutahaco
(Isleta)

• Piros
(Socorro)

APACHE DE XILA
(tcihene)

JUMANOS

MANSOS

JOCOMES
JANOS

SUMAS

N

PUEBLOS AND NOMADIC TRIBES IN 1541

0   40   80
miles

15. PUEBLOS AND NOMADIC TRIBES, 1541

WHEN THE SPANIARDS first arrived in New Mexico, they found a number of different Indian tribes living within the borders of the present state. Most important were the "Pueblo" Indians, so-called because the Spaniards were impressed with the towns in which they lived. These natives had probably been living in their current stage of civilization for about five hundred years before the Spaniards arrived, and there is ample evidence that their forefathers had settled in New Mexico countless centuries before that.

These pueblos, or rather clusters of pueblos, were primarily concentrated in the upper Río Grande Valley, with only Cíbola, Acoma, and a few settlements along the Pecos to be found very far from that river. They varied in number from about 100 people to a maximum of 2,000, the total for all of the pueblos possibly being as high as 20,000. Although their habits, customs, and traditions were very similar, these New Mexican Indians actually had different origins and spoke several different tongues.

Located in the western portion of the state was the Zuñian group. They inhabited the much sought "Seven Cities of Cíbola," which were to be such a disappointment to the Spanish. The Keres group included Acoma, the famous rich fortress, Chía, Quirix, and San Felipe. The Towa included Jèmes and Cicúique; the Tiwa, Braba, and Tutahaco; the Tewa, Yuque-Yuque. The basis of their sedentary economy was agriculture, their social and political institutions being among the more advanced of any group of natives in the United States.

Coronado and his men commented on the nomadic Indians they encountered in 1541; but, for obvious reasons, information about them is much more limited than information about the Pueblos. Because of their roving proclivities, it is difficult to be sure where the nomads were at any certain time. Most forceful of these natives were the Athapascans. Of this group the Navahos who were found in the northwestern portion of the state played a leading role in New Mexican history. The Apaches, who were also Athapascan, dominated the High Plains from Wyoming south to Texas in 1541 and were mainly found in northeastern New Mexico. Some branches of this tribe, the Apaches de Xila, were found west of the Río Grande at this early date, and ultimately different branches of the Apaches were to be found in most of the state. The Jumanos, whom Cabeza de Vaca had termed "People of the Cows," dominated the southeastern portion of the state. Their economy was based on the buffalo, and they apparently preyed upon the Apaches. Of lesser significance were the Mansos, Sumas, and Janos.

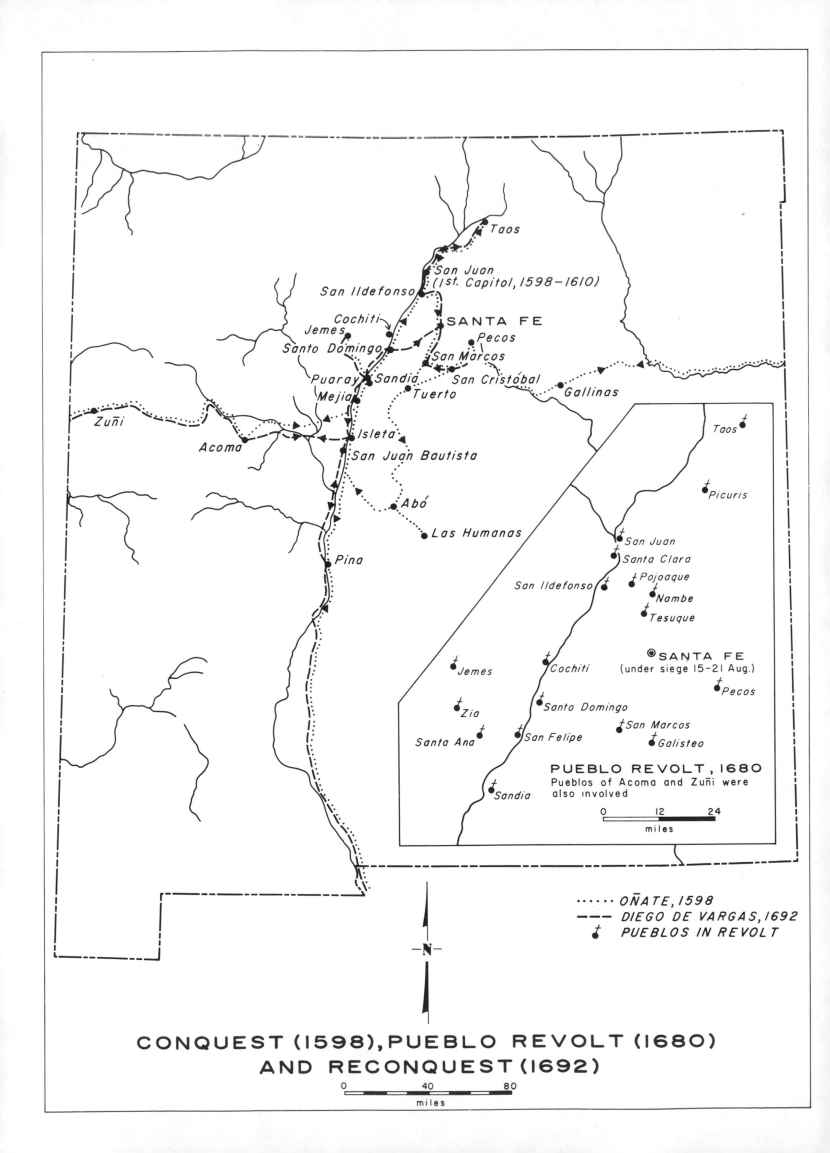

Taos

San Juan
(1st. Capitol, 1598–1610)

San Ildefonso

Cochiti
Jemes
Santo Domingo

SANTA FE

Pecos

San Marcos

Puaray Sandia
Mejia

San Cristóbal

Tuerto

Gallinas

Zuñi

Acoma

Isleta

San Juan Bautista

Abó

Las Humanas

Pina

Taos

Picuris

San Juan
Santa Clara
Pojoaque
San Ildefonso
Nambe
Tesuque

SANTA FE
(under siege 15–21 Aug.)

Jemes

Cochiti

Pecos

Zia

Santo Domingo

Santa Ana

San Felipe

San Marcos
Galisteo

PUEBLO REVOLT, 1680
Pueblos of Acoma and Zuñi were
also involved

Sandia

0   12   24
miles

·········· OÑATE, 1598
— — — DIEGO DE VARGAS, 1692
✝ PUEBLOS IN REVOLT

—N—

CONQUEST (1598), PUEBLO REVOLT (1680)
AND RECONQUEST (1692)

0   40   80
miles

16. CONQUEST, PUEBLO REVOLT, AND RECONQUE

ESPEJO'S REPORT ON MINES in New Mexico, and the abortive colonization attempt by De Sosa led to the conquest of the area in 1598 by Don Juan de Oñate. Although the Spaniards were there primarily to exploit the mineral wealth, at the same time they set about to convert the natives to Christianity.

Oñate's expedition reached the Río Grande south of the present site of El Paso and followed that river north to the Indian pueblos. Establishing his headquarters initially at San Juan, Oñate visited and conquered all of the Indian towns. The most serious opposition came from the Acoma Indians. Once the natives were pacified, the conquerors explored widely for gold and silver, going as far east as the site of Wichita, Kansas, and as far west as the Gulf of California.

Oñate established Spanish colonies which had a precarious exist
the pueblos, un
Popé of San Ju
posing as the go
the Spaniards an
all. Governor Ar
the refugees sou

Fear of possib
for the souls of
motivated the Sp
Vargas headed the army of the reconquest up the traditional route along the Río Grande. The unity displayed by the pueblos in 1680 had disintegrated after their victory, and once Vargas had recaptured Santa Fe, the remainder of the reconquest was relatively easy.

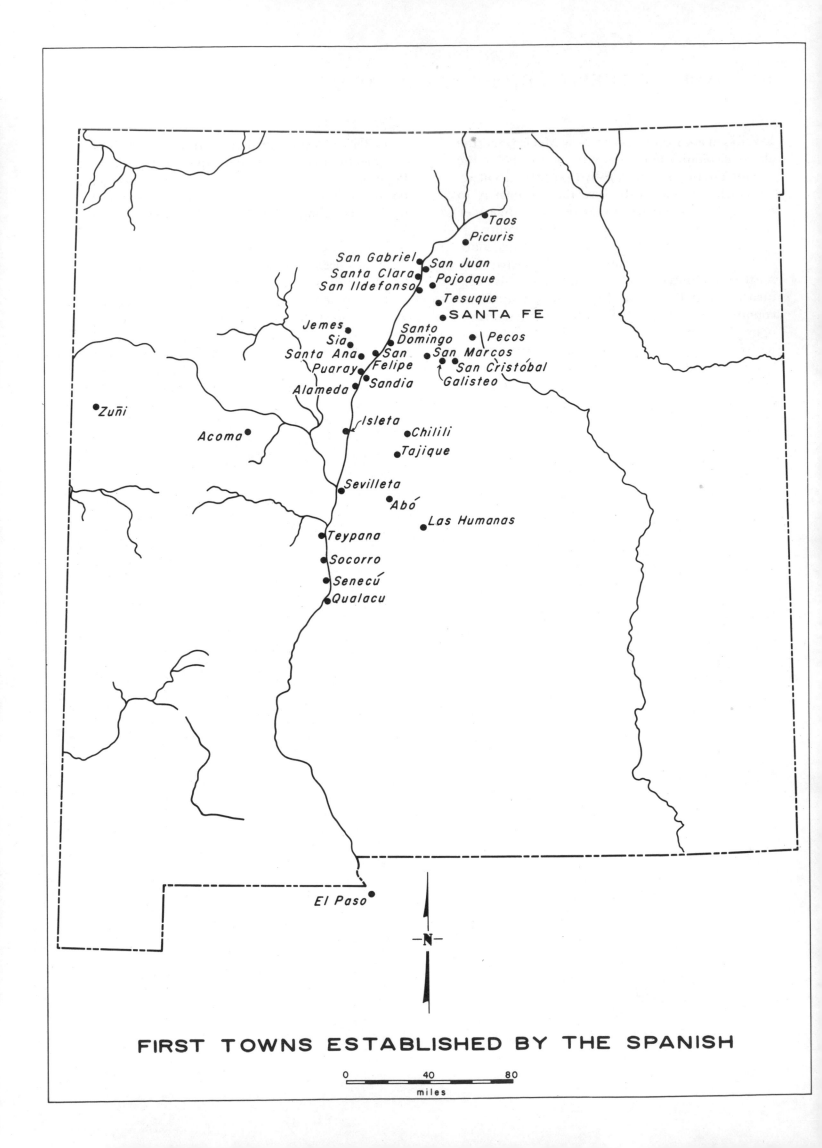

Taos
Picuris
San Gabriel
Santa Clara
San Ildefonso
San Juan
Pojoaque
Tesuque
SANTA FE
Jemes
Sia
Santo
Domingo
Pecos
Santa Ana
Puaray
San
Felipe
San Marcos
San Cristóbal
Alameda
Sandia
Galisteo
Zuñi
Isleta
Chilili
Acoma
Tajique
Sevilleta
Abó
Las Humanas
Teypana
Socorro
Senecú
Qualacu
El Paso
-N-

FIRST TOWNS ESTABLISHED BY THE SPANISH

0   40   80
miles

17. FIRST TOWNS

DURING THE SEVENTEENTH CENTURY, Spanish control of New Mexico was limited to the Río Grande Valley from Qualacu on the south to Taos on the north. West of the river, control was maintained over Zuñi and Acoma, and Spanish domination extended to Pecos on the east. A few exceptions were settlements such as Abó and Las Humanas.

In restricting their area of settlement, the Spaniards followed the pattern established by the sedentary Indians before their arrival. Native towns had been limited to the same area, where land and water were available for farming and hostile Indians were less likely to attack. Not until the early eighteenth century did Spanish settlers expand their area of settlement to any extent.

The Spanish towns were grouped together along the Río Grande for easy communication with Mexico. At the time of the Pueblo Revolt of 1680, only about 2,500 Spaniards were in the area. Spanish control was basically a religious affair, with one or two clergy and a few soldiers stationed at the Indian pueblos. Since native labor was the primary economic resource of the territory, locating Spanish towns adjacent to Indian pueblos was profitable. By means of the encomienda, Spaniards forced the Indians to labor in their fields and workshops.

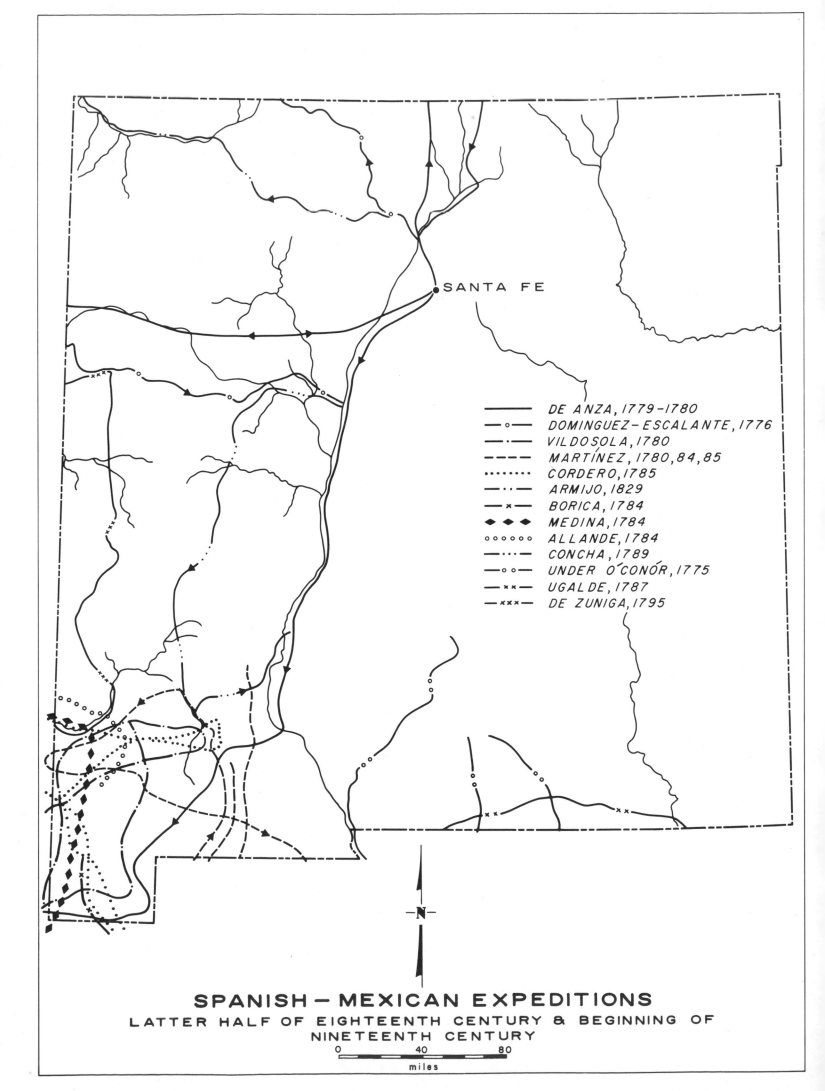

SANTA FE

DE ANZA, 1779-1780
DOMINGUEZ-ESCALANTE, 1776
VILDOSOLA, 1780
MARTINEZ, 1780, 84, 85
CORDERO, 1785
ARMIJO, 1829
BORICA, 1784
MEDINA, 1784
ALLANDE, 1784
CONCHA, 1789
UNDER O'CONÓR, 1775
UGALDE, 1787
DE ZUNIGA, 1795

N

SPANISH—MEXICAN EXPEDITIONS
LATTER HALF OF EIGHTEENTH CENTURY & BEGINNING OF NINETEENTH CENTURY

0   40   80

miles

18. SPANISH-MEXICAN EXPEDITIONS

IN THE LATTER PART of the eighteenth and beginning of the nineteenth centuries, there were many exploratory expeditions in New Mexico. There were several reasons for this renewed activity. First of all, as part of the changed Spanish defense policy, foreigners were forbidden to settle in areas under the flag of Madrid. California had been colonized under this policy, and it was absolutely necessary to find an acceptable route between the Pacific coast and Santa Fe, neither the ocean route nor the one across the Sonora Desert being satisfactory. It was also desirable to link the new missions at Tucson with Santa Fe.

During this period, interest in Indian conversion was renewed. The desire to save the souls of the Moquis, for example, motivated several expeditions. Military campaigns against the Apaches led to much exploration in the southwestern portion of the state. Renewed interest in trade on the part of individuals accounted for much other activity. One aspect of commerce between the Spanish-Mexicans and the Indians was the slave trade. In some respects this was a continuation of the earlier thrust outward of the Spanish frontier in quest of an always needed labor supply.

Trade with Indians in the Great Basin led to successful explorations by Fathers Sylvestre Veles de Escalante and Francisco Atanasio Dominguez in 1776. The much sought after California route was not found, but communication with the north became relatively common after this date. Establishing imperial connections to the southwest was easier, and several expeditions made their way from Tucson to Santa Fe. It has even been reported that Californians were trading with the New Mexico capital by 1809.

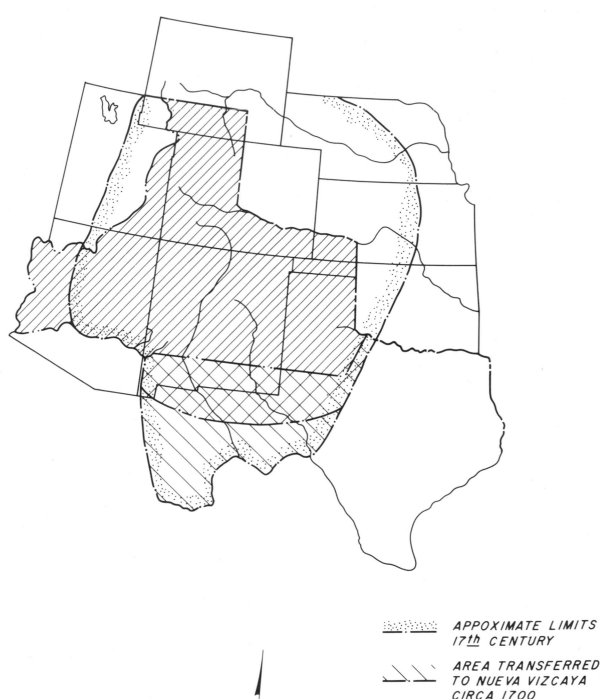

N

THE BOUNDARIES OF NEW MEXICO
DURING THE SPANISH AND MEXICAN PERIODS

0   100   200   300   400   500
miles

19. THE BOUNDARIES OF NEW MEXICO DURING THE SPANISH AND MEXICAN PERIODS

THROUGHOUT MOST OF THIS PERIOD the limits of the territory of New Mexico were ill-defined. This was to Spain's advantage, for if no exact boundaries were set, she could lay claim to the vast area north of Mexico which was still *tierra incognita*.

When Don Juan de Oñate was granted a concession to colonize New Mexico, this cut off the indefinite northern jurisdiction of Nueva Vizcaya. Unfortunately, the location of the boundary line between the two provinces was not specified in the contract and would be a matter of dispute for years. The boundaries between these two Spanish provinces were only vaguely defined, because precise limits were unnecessary so long as the frontier settlements of the respective provinces were widely separated. The establishment in 1659 of a settlement at the strategic river crossing of El Paso del Norte led to the initial conflict. After the reconquest by Diego de Vargas (about 1700), the El Paso settlements and substantial territory were transferred from New Mexico to the jurisdiction of Nueva Vizcaya. During the eighteenth century much conflict took place on the eastern limits of the vast area known as New Mexico because of French encroachment. An armed clash in what is today the state of Nebraska resulted. This threat was eliminated in 1763 when France ceded the Louisiana Territory to Spain.

Purchase of Louisiana Territory by the United States from France in 1803 caused a boundary conflict between the United States and Spain. This friction was one of the reasons for the expedition into New Mexico by Zebulon Pike and almost resulted in an armed clash along the Sabine River in East Texas. The Adams-Onís Treaty of 1819 settled this phase of the boundary controversy. The line agreed upon was fixed at the Sabine River to 32° North Latitude, thence due north to the Red River. It followed that river west to 100° West Longitude, north on that line to the Arkansas River, westward up that stream to its source, north to the 42nd parallel of North Latitude, and westward to the Pacific Ocean.

After Mexico had obtained her independence from Spain, the boundary was again revised in 1824. The Province of Nueva Vizcaya was divided into two new provinces, Chihuahua and Durango. The new boundaries gave the state of Chihuahua a portion of southern New Mexico and a large part of the present state of Texas.

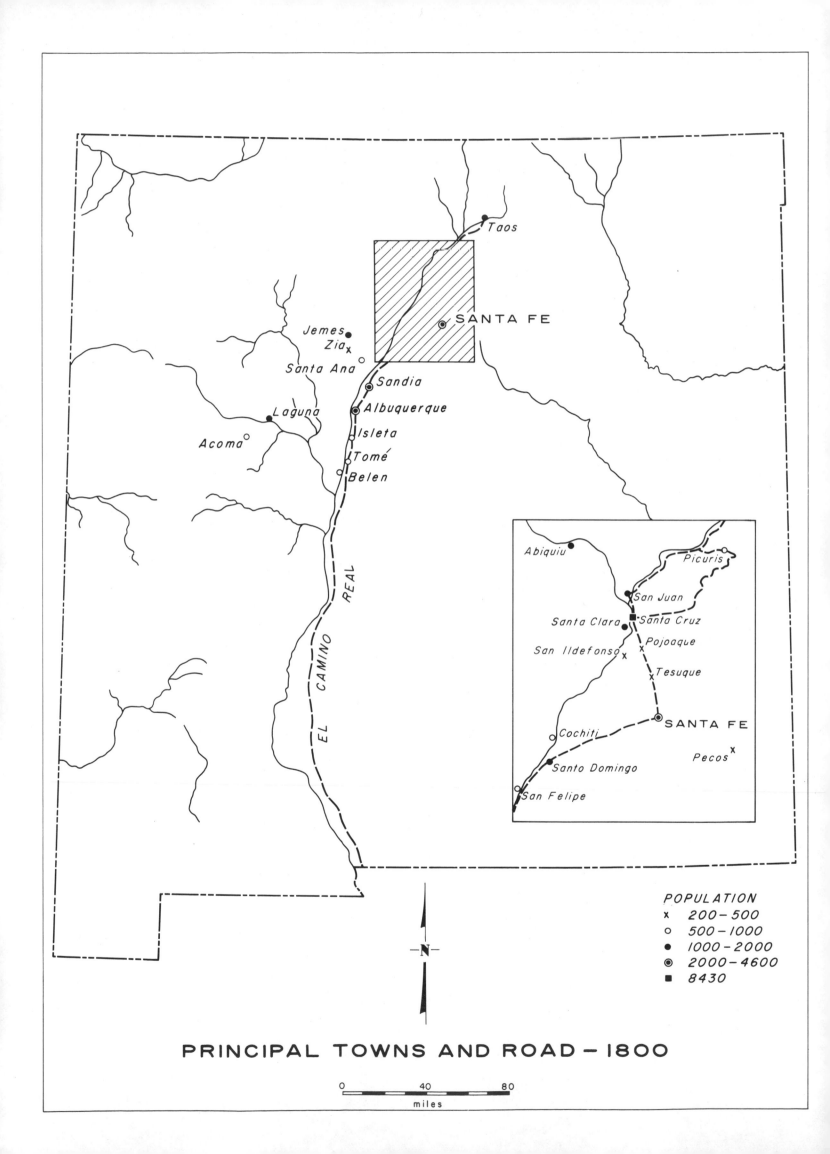

Taos

Jemes
Zia ×
Santa Ana °

Sandia ◉
Albuquerque ◉
Isleta °
Tomé °
Belen °

Laguna ●

Acoma °

SANTA FE ◉

EL CAMINO REAL

Abiquiu ●
Picuris °
San Juan ●
Santa Clara ●   Santa Cruz ■
San Ildefonso ×   Pojoaque ×
Tesuque ×
SANTA FE ◉
Cochiti °
Pecos ×
Santo Domingo ●
San Felipe °

POPULATION
×   200–500
°   500–1000
●   1000–2000
◉   2000–4600
■   8430

—N—

PRINCIPAL TOWNS AND ROAD – 1800

0   40   80
miles

20. PRINCIPAL TOWNS AND ROAD, 1800

BY 1800, THE SPANISH TOWNS of New Mexico had changed only slightly from the pattern established earlier. Fear of attack by hostile natives after the uprising of 1680 continued to dictate a concentration of population along the banks of the upper Río Grande or its adjacent tributaries. Then too, Spaniards always preferred the town to a strictly rural environment, and in an alien and hostile land they were reluctant to move far from protection or the arteries of trade linking New Mexico to the center of civilization in Mexico City.

There were, however, certain forces at work causing some slow but inevitable changes in settlement. First of all, the reconquest by Diego de Vargas in the 1690's had caused the depopulation of many pueblos and thus made available improved lands which Spaniards appropriated for their own use.

As the population in New Mexico increased, more distant lands had to be utilized. Thus, land grants were obtained on the tributaries of the Río Grande, frequently far from existing settlements, in spite of the constant danger of attack by the Comanches and Apaches.

Albuquerque, founded in 1706, Sandia, Santa Fe, and Santa Cruz remained the centers of population. By 1800 there were 18,826 Spaniards and 9,732 Pueblo Indians in the territory. The trail along the Río Grande, known as El Camino Real, continued to link the isolated frontier communities with the centers of authority in Mexico. Wool and hides were the main items of commerce shipped southward, but in general most New Mexicans were as self-sufficient as they had been when the settlements were first established two centuries before.

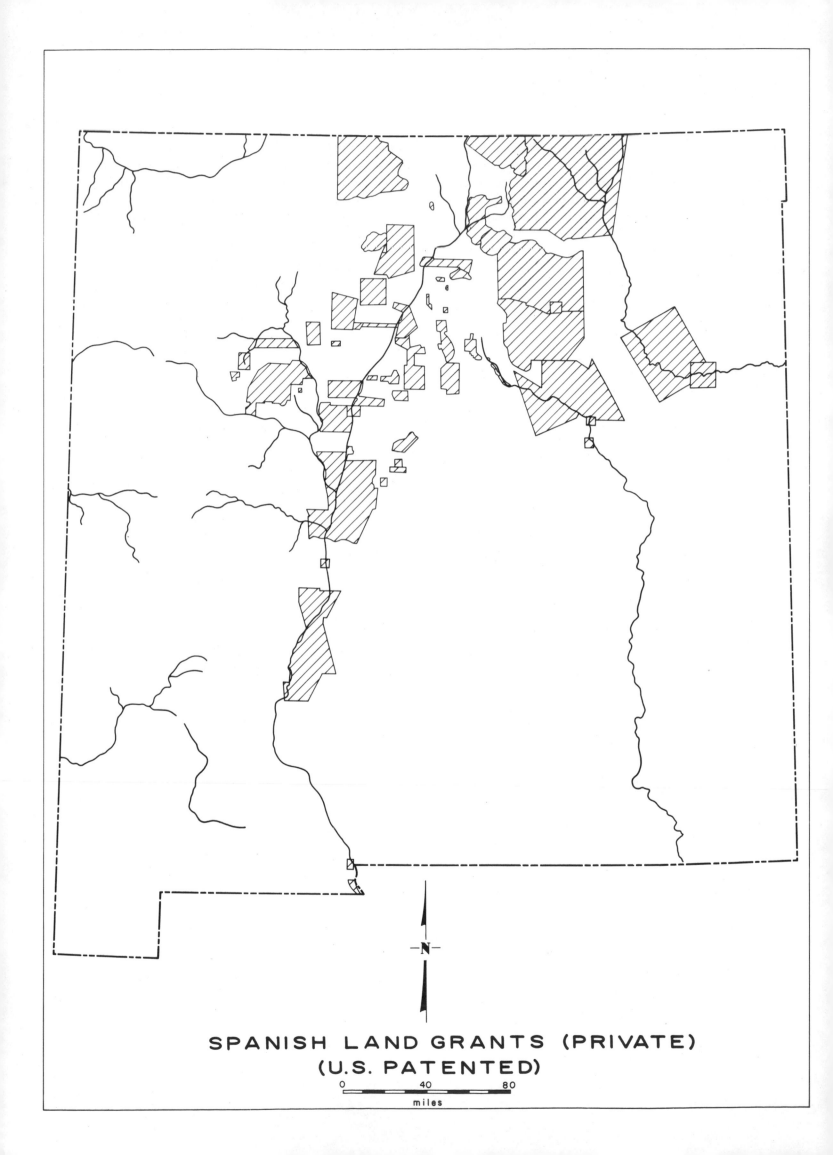

SPANISH LAND GRANTS (PRIVATE)
(U.S. PATENTED)

0   40   80

miles

21. SPANISH LAND GRANTS

THE LAND GRANT SYSTEM originated with the Spanish practice of granting large areas of land to individuals or groups for meritorious service to the Crown or for various other reasons. New Mexico had been settled for about two and one-half centuries before the coming of the Anglo-Americans, so it was inevitable that the best land along the streams had long since been granted by the Spanish and Mexican governments. These grants were protected in the Treaty of 1848. Unfortunately, there had been a great deal of careless informality regarding title papers so that the boundaries of the grants were usually vague, and the grants themselves had become complicated by frequent transfers and subdivisions. In addition, the records of such grants were usually inaccurate and, in many cases, were even missing.

Uncertainty as to the validity of land titles ob-viously would hamper the development of the territory. In 1854, Congress provided for a surveyor general to pass on the validity of the land titles in question, Congress making the final disposition. An office understaffed to perform the necessary duties, a native population which did not understand what was at stake, and politics made for a situation in which fraud and injustice were all too common.

By 1886, of the original 205 land claims filed, 13 were rejected, 141 were approved, and the remaining 51 had not been acted upon. In 1891, Congress established a "Court of Private Land Claims" in an effort to remove the complex issue from the political arena. By the time this court completed its work in 1904, it had heard suits concerning 35,491,020 acres. Claims confirmed by decrees of the court involved only 2,051,526 acres. Claims rejected involved 33,439,493 acres.

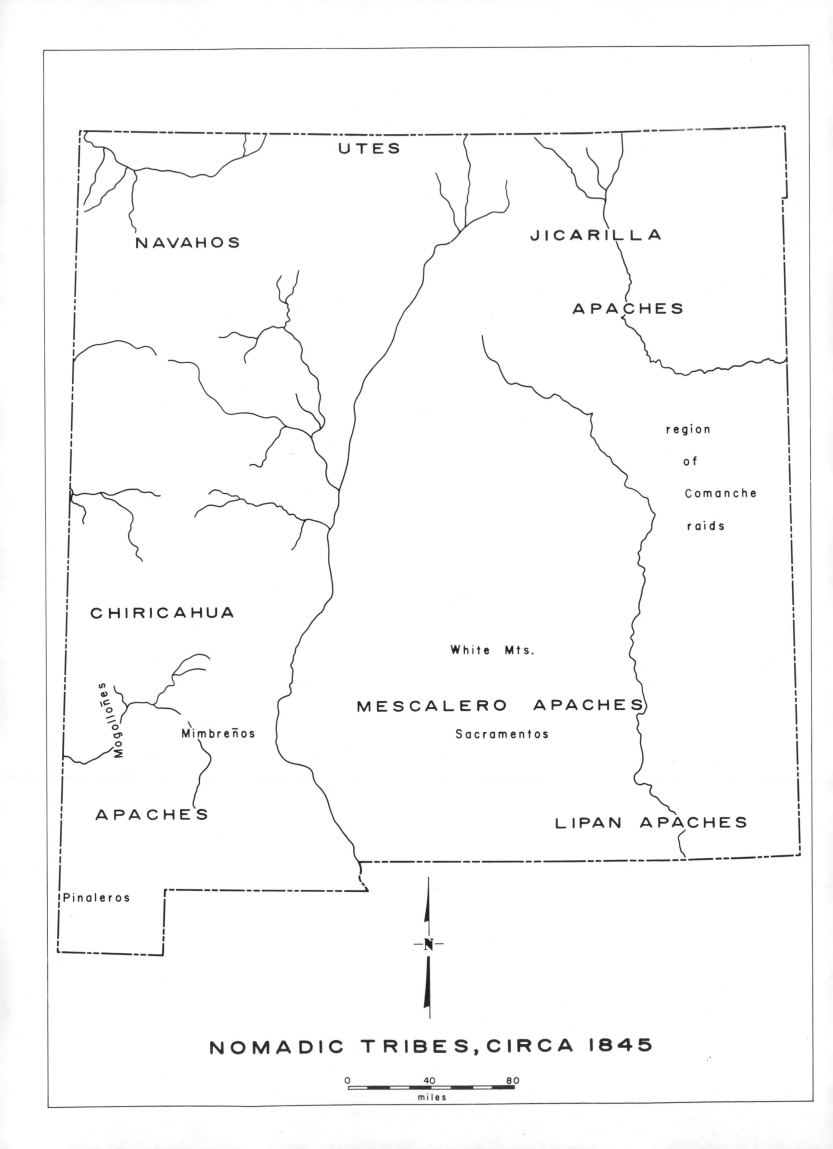

UTES

NAVAHOS

JICARILLA

APACHES

region

of

Comanche

raids

CHIRICAHUA

White Mts.

MESCALERO APACHES

Mogollones

Sacramentos

Mimbreños

APACHES

LIPAN APACHES

Pinaleros

N

NOMADIC TRIBES, CIRCA 1845

0   40   80
miles

MANY NOMADIC TRIBES were based primarily in New Mexico, but their wanderings frequently took them far from the present boundaries of the state. These natives had drifted southward through the years for a variety of reasons. Some had undoubtedly fled to the mountains of New Mexico because of drought in their native habitat or because more warlike tribes had driven them there to seek refuge. Most of these Indians were Apaches and members of the Athapascan family. Years of living in the semiarid country had taught the Apaches to adjust to a difficult natural environment. In fact, they had evolved into one of the toughest human species the world had ever known. This "Arab of the New World" held sway over a vast part of the Southwest which the Spaniards called Apacheria. Ostensibly, Mexico controlled New Mexico in 1845. In actual fact, as the United States was soon to discover, a few miles away from the Río Grande and its tributaries the Apaches roamed with relative freedom. Many campaigns by Spain and Mexico in the century preceding 1845 had failed to break the spirit of these superb warriors.

The Navahos, really a branch of the Apaches, were the largest group in the area in 1845, just as they are in the second half of the twentieth century. Spanish sources confirm that the Navahos were in northwestern New Mexico by 1706 and have since remained in control of this region. They raised corn and livestock, and successively raided the Pueblo Indians and the Spanish settlements, so that for almost a century and a half a monotonous succession of campaigns was launched against them to no avail.

The Mescalero Apaches inhabited the Guadalupes, the Sierra Blanca, and the Davis Mountains, although they did roam eastward across the plains. The Indians were so named because mescal was their staple food. The Jicarilla Apaches (named after the baskets they wove) were found in northeastern New Mexico and were not considered equal to other Apaches as warriors. The Chiricahua Apaches in the southwestern corner of the state, however, made up in military prowess what the Jicarillas lacked.

The non-Apache nomadic tribes were both on the periphery of New Mexico. The Utes roamed southward into the northern portion of the state from their home base in Colorado. They were allied with and frequently intermarried with the Jicarillas. The Comanches were a Plains tribe whose economy was built around the buffalo. They came southward from Wyoming in the eighteenth century, and once they acquired the horse, they dominated the southern Great Plains. They alternately raided and traded with the New Mexican settlements of Spanish or Indian pueblos. Both the Utes and Comanches were from the Shoshonean family.

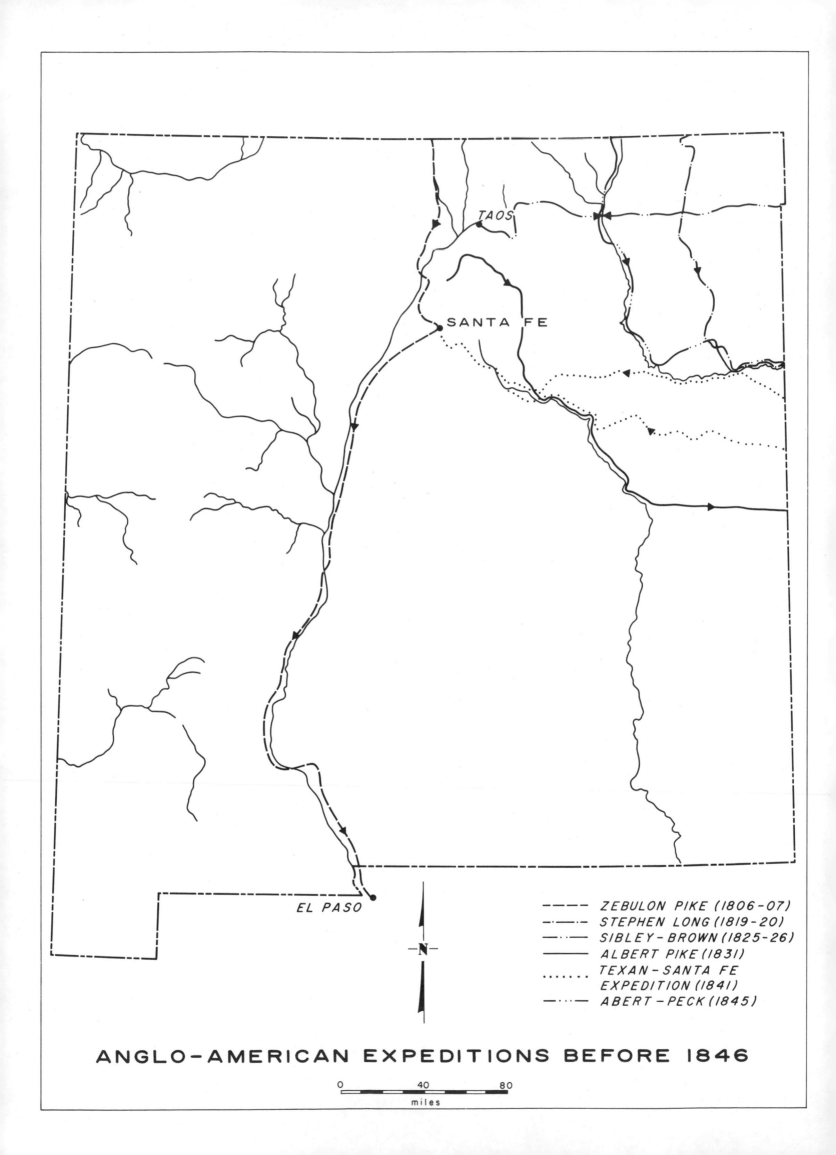

TAOS

SANTA FE

EL PASO

—N—

- - - - - - - ZEBULON PIKE (1806-07)
- · - · - · - STEPHEN LONG (1819-20)
— ·· — ·· — SIBLEY-BROWN (1825-26)
——————— ALBERT PIKE (1831)
· · · · · · · TEXAN-SANTA FE
EXPEDITION (1841)
— ··· — ··· — ABERT-PECK (1845)

ANGLO-AMERICAN EXPEDITIONS BEFORE 1846

0   40   80
miles

IN THE YEARS PRECEDING the Mexican War, Anglo-American expeditions found their way into New Mexico. The reasons for this transit through Mexican territory varied. Lieutenant Zebulon Pike claimed to have been "lost." Others had scientific purposes. But most of the trespassers had some connection with the flourishing trade along the Santa Fe Trail.

Lieutenant Pike was the first of the intruders into New Mexico, and the reasons for his action were so devious that historians are still unsure of them. After constructing a blockhouse on the Río Grande near the mouth of the Río Conejos, the American, with his companions, was captured by the Spaniards. They were not released until they had been escorted down the Río Grande and eventually to Chihuahua. The most important result of this episode was that the youthful Pike was a most competent observer, and his published journal attracted many more Americans, especially fur trappers and traders, to New Mexico.

Major Stephen H. Long's scientific exploratory venture into the northeastern corner of the state in 1820 probably occurred because the boundary in the plains country was vague.

Opening of the Santa Fe trade in 1821 caused the United States government to seek the best route from Missouri to New Mexico. In 1825–26, George C. Sibley led a United States commission which marked a road from Fort Osage to Taos that was seldom, if ever, used by the traders. In 1831, Albert Pike traversed the Llano Estacado en route eastward to Fort Smith, Arkansas, but his route was one few others tried to follow.

In 1841 the ill-fated Texan–Santa Fe Expedition made its way across the inhospitable plains, meaning to share in the lucrative Santa Fe trade. Instead of gaining a monetary reward, however, the Texans were captured and rudely treated as invaders.

Lieutenants James William Abert and William G. Peck of the Topographical Engineers were commissioned to make an extensive trip through New Mexico to collect data so the government would have a better idea of this area. Their exploration was the precursor of the many scientific expeditions carried out in New Mexico by the United States Army in the 1850's.

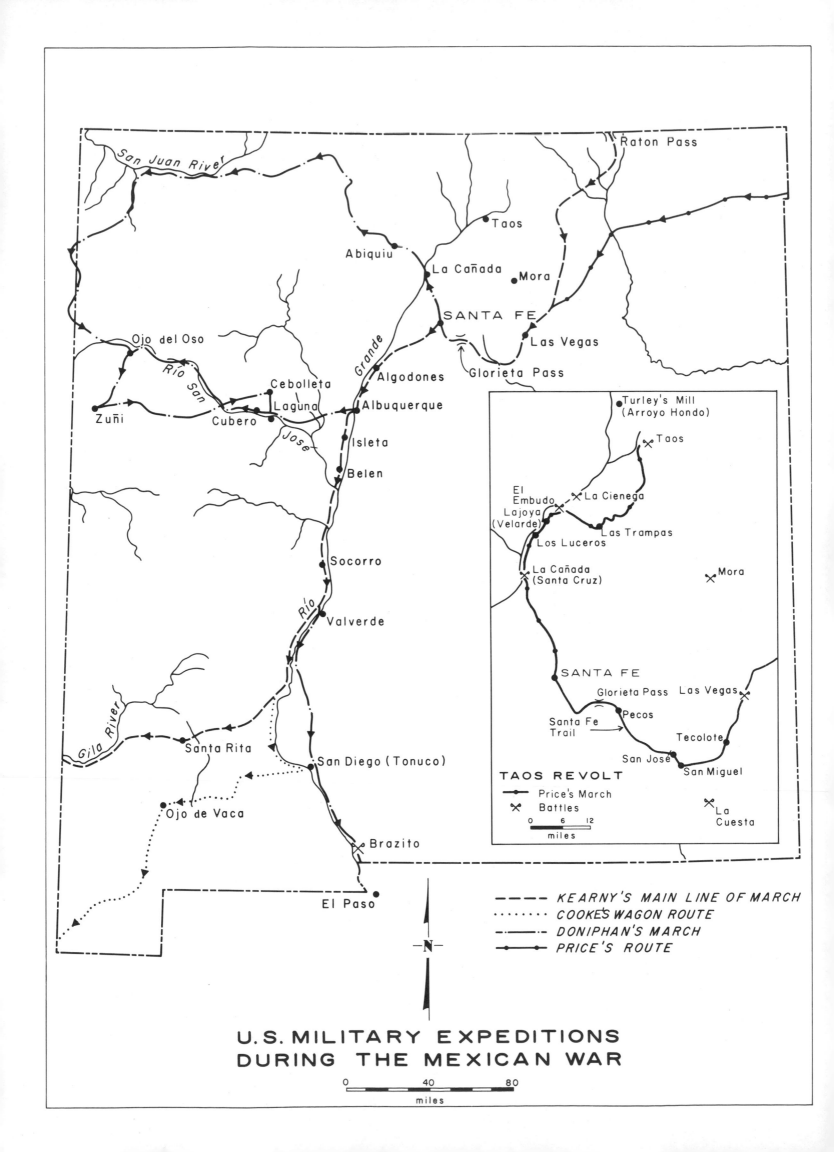

San Juan River

Raton Pass

Taos

Abiquiu

La Cañada

Mora

SANTA FE

Las Vegas

Ojo del Oso

Glorieta Pass

Río San

Grande

Algodones

Cebolleta

Laguna

Albuquerque

Zuñi

Cubero

Jose

Isleta

Belen

Socorro

Río

Valverde

Gila River

Santa Rita

San Diego (Tonuco)

Ojo de Vaca

Brazito

El Paso

TAOS REVOLT

Turley's Mill
(Arroyo Hondo)

Taos

El Embudo

La Cienega

Lajoya
(Velarde)

Las Trampas

Los Luceros

La Cañada
(Santa Cruz)

Mora

SANTA FE

Glorieta Pass

Las Vegas

Santa Fe
Trail

Pecos

Tecolote

San José

San Miguel

La
Cuesta

●———— Price's March
✕ Battles

0   6   12
▬▬▬▬▬▬▬
miles

– – – KEARNY'S MAIN LINE OF MARCH
· · · · · COOKE'S WAGON ROUTE
–·–·– DONIPHAN'S MARCH
●—●— PRICE'S ROUTE

N

U.S. MILITARY EXPEDITIONS
DURING THE MEXICAN WAR

0   40   80
▬▬▬▬▬▬▬▬▬▬▬▬▬
miles

24. UNITED STATES MILITARY EXPEDITIONS DURING THE MEXICAN WAR

New Mexico was not a scene of major battles during the Mexican War, but a few skirmishes did take place within its borders. The main invading army under General Stephen Watts Kearny entered via the mountain route of the Santa Fe Trail. At Glorieta Pass the Mexican forces failed to resist as expected, and the Americans marched into Santa Fe. Believing the war in New Mexico to be over, Kearny left for California with only a small number of troops. Colonel Philip St. George Cooke was detached from the main force for the purpose of blazing a wagon trail to the West Coast. The Mormon Battalion under his command went through Guadalupe Pass into Arizona, and the route they charted was to later become a much-traveled road to California.

After marching into the northwestern corner of the state and returning to the Río Grande via Zuñi, Colonel Alexander William Doniphan's Missouri Volunteers left for the Mexican battlefields. At Brazito on the lower Río Grande the Volunteers were attacked by a Mexican detachment, which they defeated.

In January, 1847, an uprising occurred in Taos, taking the life of Governor Charles Bent, among others. Americans were also killed at Arroyo Hondo and Mora. An army under Colonel Sterling Price, marching from Santa Fe, met and routed the rebels at La Cañada. Another engagement at El Embudo caused the Mexican force to retreat to the pueblo at Taos. The Americans besieged the enemy in the pueblo and ultimately captured most of them. Skirmishes occurred later at La Cuesta, Las Vegas, and La Cienega near Taos.

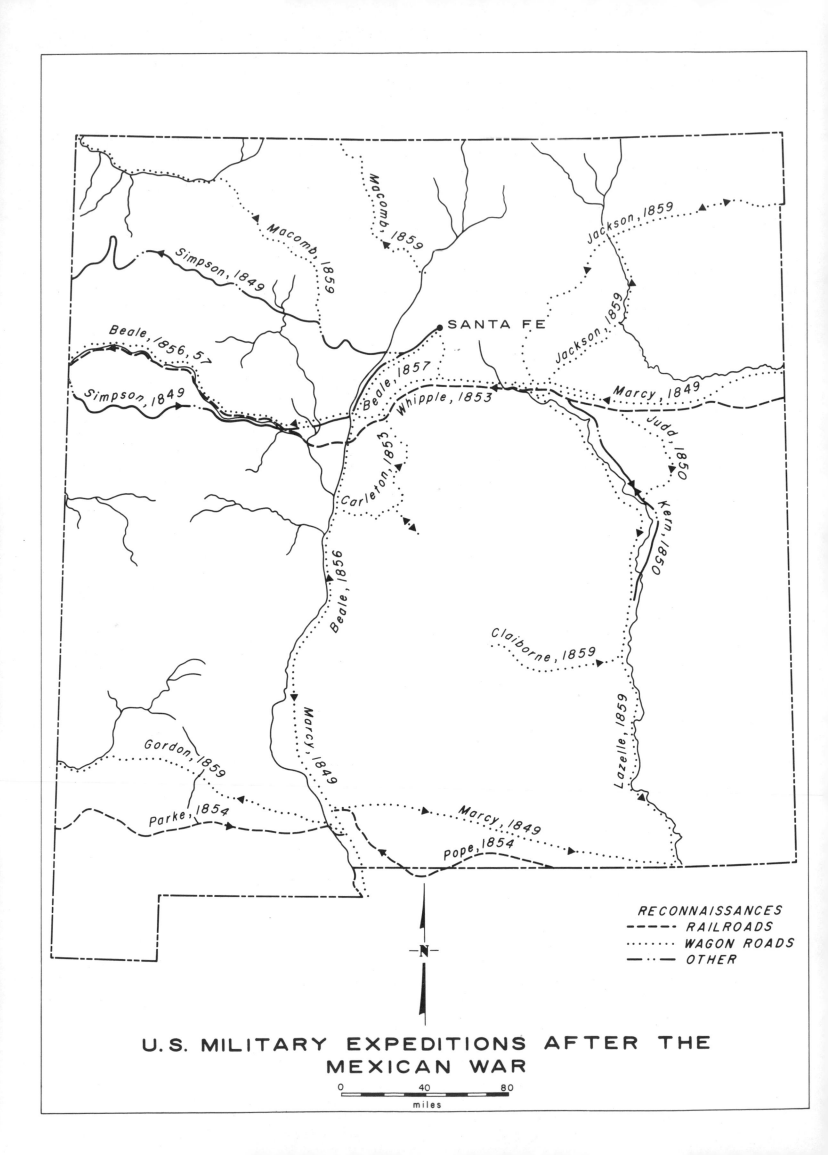

SANTA FE

Macomb, 1859

Macomb, 1859

Jackson, 1859

Jackson, 1859

Simpson, 1849

Beale, 1856, 57

Simpson, 1849

Beale, 1857

Whipple, 1853

Marcy, 1849

Judd, 1850

Carleton, 1853

Kern, 1850

Beale, 1856

Claiborne, 1859

Lazelle, 1859

Marcy, 1849

Gordon, 1859

Parke, 1854

Marcy, 1849

Pope, 1854

RECONNAISSANCES
- - - - *RAILROADS*
· · · · · *WAGON ROADS*
-·-·- *OTHER*

-N-

U.S. MILITARY EXPEDITIONS AFTER THE MEXICAN WAR

0   40   80

miles

25. UNITED STATES MILITARY EXPEDITIONS AFTER THE MEXICAN WAR

IN THE YEARS BETWEEN the end of the Mexican War and the beginning of the Civil War, the United States Army made fifteen official exploratory expeditions within the territory of New Mexico. The basic purpose of these ventures was to provide the government with detailed information about the area acquired from Mexico.

First of all, the explorations were scientific in nature and provided information about the topography, the flora and fauna, and especially the Indians. The presence of these army expeditions was intended to impress the nomadic and the hostile Indians with the power of the federal government. Some of these were punitive campaigns. Others were for the purpose of negotiating treaties. The soldiers sought out suitable locations for forts and charted roads and trails that could be used for military purposes.

When gold was discovered in California, the consequent migration to the Pacific coast made some form of transcontinental transportation system a national necessity. Hence, many of the army expeditions surveyed possible roads and railroad routes. Finally, the army helped survey the Mexico–New Mexico boundary.

During these military expeditions, most of New Mexico was effectively mapped, and the scientific data gathered then has remained of value to those interested in the Southwest. These explorations made way for the stagecoach and the railroad, which in turn made easier the influx of miners, ranchers, and farmers in the post–Civil War period.

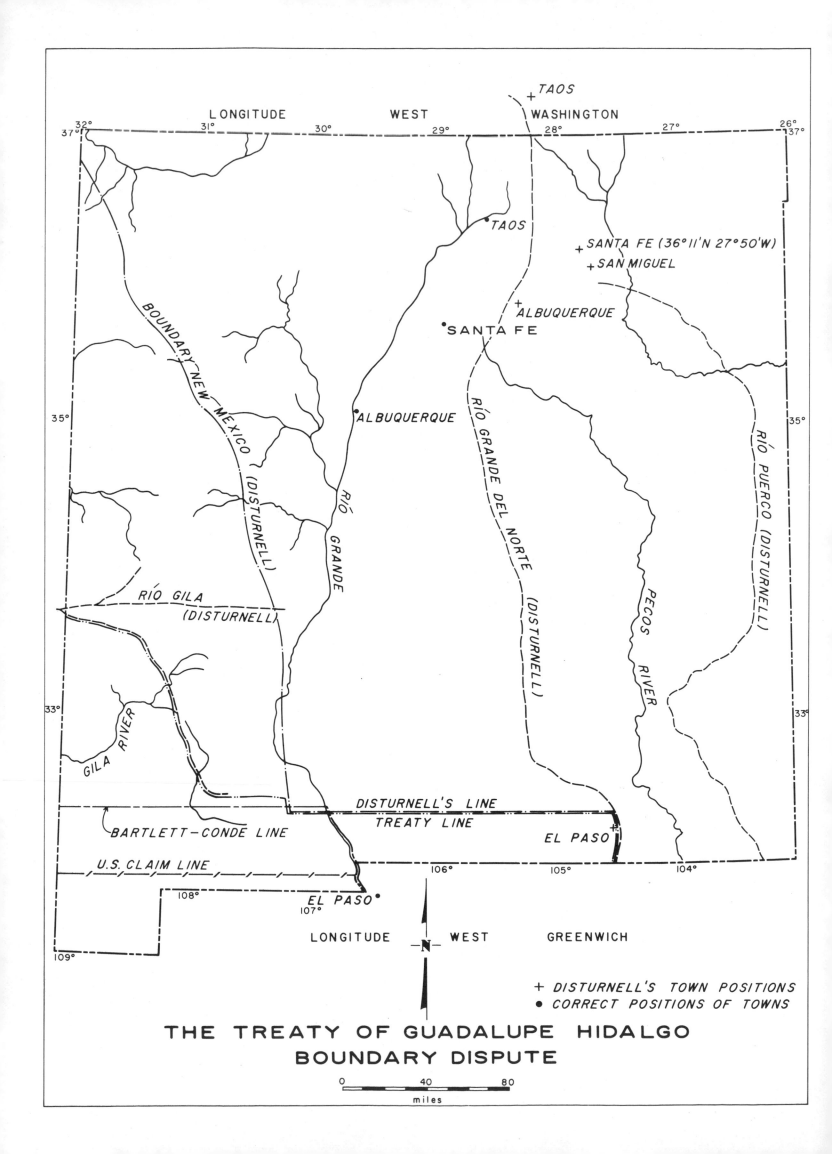

THE TREATY OF GUADALUPE HIDALGO
BOUNDARY DISPUTE

26. THE TREATY OF GUADALUPE HIDALGO BOUNDARY DISPUTE

THE EXACT LOCATION of the southern boundary between Mexico and New Mexico was in dispute for several years because the Disturnell map was incorporated into the Treaty of Guadalupe Hidalgo. That treaty provided: "The southern and western limits of New Mexico, mentioned in this article, are those laid down in the map . . . published in New York in 1847 by J. Disturnell." The boundary line between New Mexico (and what is now Arizona) and Old Mexico was based on mileages from El Paso. The controversy arose because the Disturnell map showed El Paso at a latitude 34 miles north and a longitude 100 miles east of the true position of that city.

The most valuable areas in dispute were the good farming land available in the Mesilla Valley, the copper mines at Santa Rita in what is today southwestern New Mexico, and the Gila River Valley, a possible southern railroad route. The Disturnell map showed a line starting about 8 miles above El Paso, running west 3° of longitude, then running north to the Gila. Unfortunately, El Paso on the map and El Paso on the earth were in two different locations. According to the map, the east-west boundary of New Mexico started 8 miles above El Paso, or 8 miles above the latitude and longitude shown for El Paso on the map. But, in reality, the east-west boundary started from the Río Grande about 42 miles north of El Paso. The north-south line was inaccurate on the map too. This was supposed to be 3° of longitude west of El Paso. But the map showed El Paso 100 miles east of its true location.

The treaty negotiators had foreseen some possible disagreements and had provided for a commission representing both governments to designate the proper boundary with due precision. John Russell Bartlett represented the United States, and General Pedro Conde represented Mexico. These men quickly discovered the error in the Disturnell map, and what evolved was known as the Bartlett-Conde compromise line. Conde got the east-west line according to the map (42 miles above El Paso), and Bartlett got the north-south line by the stars (100 miles farther west than if he had gone by the map). This solution was most favorable to Mexico, for by these terms, it acquired the Mesilla Valley. Bartlett got control of the Santa Rita copper mines for the United States, but he failed to obtain the southern railroad route. Some members of the United States commission would not sanction the compromise, and late in 1852, Congress repudiated the arrangement.

Meanwhile, the possibility of a pitched conflict in the Mesilla Valley was very real. Chihuahuan officials took over the valley and decreed that no Americans could hold land there. Once Congress had repudiated the compromise, the territorial governor of New Mexico proclaimed United States' authority over the Mesilla strip, and the possibility of an armed clash was imminent. Only a suitable diplomatic move could solve the problem. The Gadsden Purchase in 1853 was to be such a move.

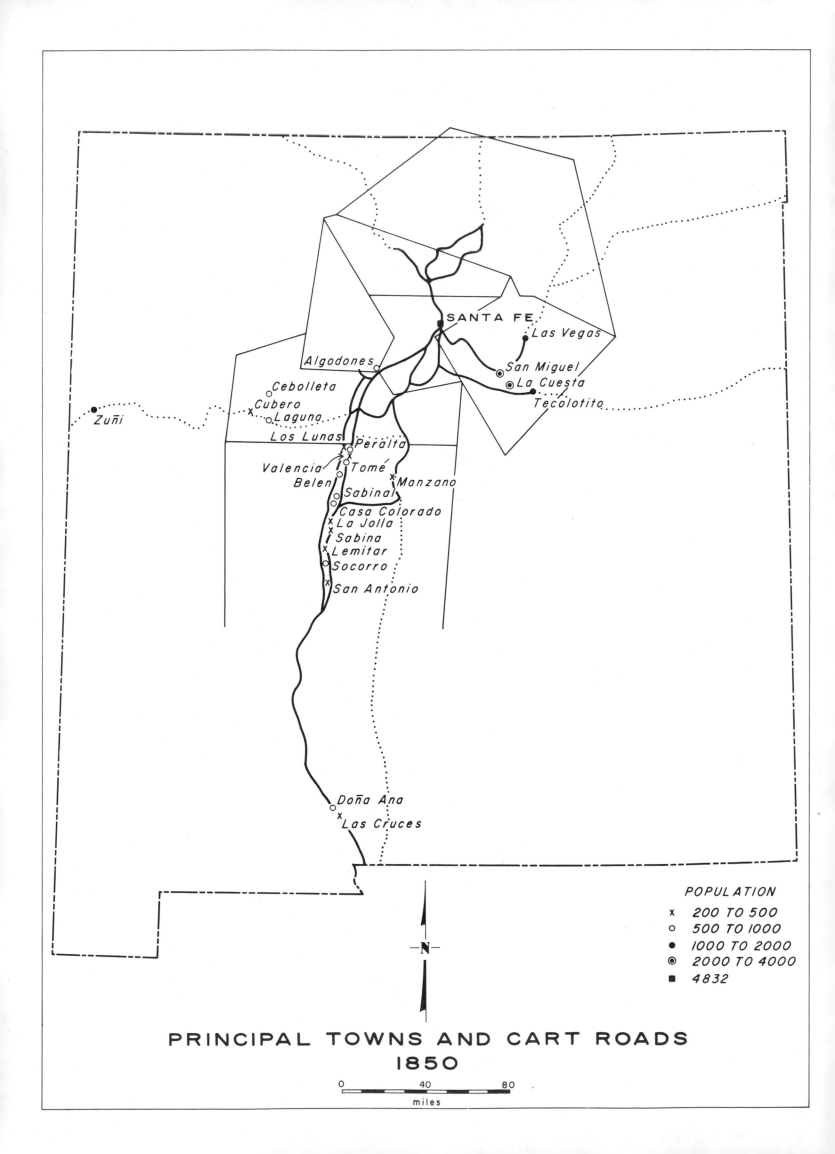

SANTA FE

Las Vegas

Algodones

San Miguel

La Cuesta

Cebolleta

Tecolotito

Cubero

Zuñi

Laguna

Los Lunas

Peralta

Valencia

Tomé

Belen

Manzano

Sabinal

Casa Colorado

La Jolla

Sabina

Lemitar

Socorro

San Antonio

Doña Ana

Las Cruces

POPULATION

x	200 TO 500
o	500 TO 1000
●	1000 TO 2000
◉	2000 TO 4000
■	4832

—N—

PRINCIPAL TOWNS AND CART ROADS
1850

0   40   80

miles

In 1850 THE POPULATION of all of the territory of New Mexico was 61,547. This total included the area which later became the territory of Arizona but did not include Indians. Even after allowing for a margin of error in the taking of the census this shows a substantial increase over the census figure of 43,433 in 1827, which included both Indians and whites.

At the midway point in the nineteenth century, New Mexico's population distribution had deviated but little from the pattern established in the long period of Spanish rule. Most of the state's inhabitants were still clustered along the Río Grande Valley or the river's tributaries. The few exceptions were found along the eastern approaches of the Santa Fe Trail or near the western pueblos. Manzano had been settled as early as 1816 and was confirmed by a grant in 1839.

Fear of hostile Indians remained the primary reason people were reluctant to leave the established settlements. When gold was discovered in 1828 in the Ortiz Mountains between Albuquerque and Santa Fe, the population spread out, at least for a time.

Cart roads used to connect the population centers had been opened by the Spaniards, or had been charted even earlier by Indians, who used them for trade. Most important of these was the Santa Fe Trail, the main trade artery of the state. All types of general consumer goods entered this route, and furs, gold, and silver made the return trip to Missouri. In the initial stages of this trade. Santa Fe was a port of entry for much of the Mexican territory. During the decade (1822–32) incoming merchandise was sent southward via "New Mexico's Royal Road," down the Río Grande into Mexico, and even overland to California. The heavy migration to the gold fields of California gave the trails westward new importance.

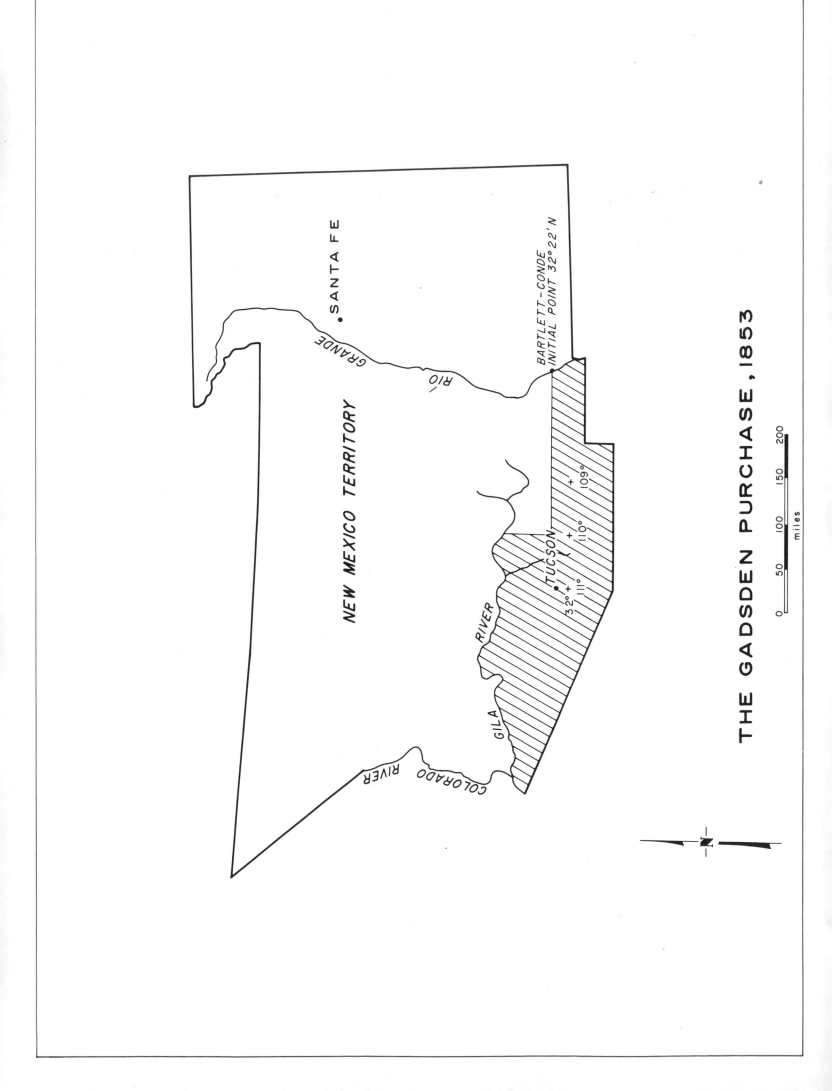

NEW MEXICO TERRITORY

• SANTA FE

RIO GRANDE

BARTLETT-CONDE
INITIAL POINT 32° 22' N

109°
+

110°
+

TUCSON

111°
+
32°
+

GILA
RIVER

COLORADO RIVER

THE GADSDEN PURCHASE, 1853

miles
0   50   100   150   200

N

28. THE GADSDEN PURCHASE, 1853

THE GADSDEN PURCHASE settled the boundary dispute resulting from the Treaty of Guadalupe Hidalgo and the inaccuracies of the Disturnell treaty map, and set a territorial limit of the United States. Southerners favored the purchase, desiring to acquire territory suitable for the southern route of a transcontinental railroad.

The purchase was negotiated by James Gadsden, a railroad executive from South Carolina. As minister to Mexico, he had learned at once that President Santa Anna's government was bankrupt. With this knowledge, he was able to successfully negotiate the Gadsden Purchase, which was signed in Mexico City on December 30, 1853.

The new boundary line started at a point on the Río Grande at 31° 47′ North Latitude and ran due west 100 miles, then due south to the parallel of 31° 20′; it continued due west on this parallel to its intersection with the 111th meridian; then it ran in a direct northwest line to a point on the Colorado River 20 miles below its confluence with the Gila;

then up the Colorado to the established boundary and west along it to the Pacific.

Because of Northern resistance to what was considered Southern designs, the Senate did not ratify the treaty until April 25, 1854. As there were delays in paying the $10,000,000 prescribed, the Mexican authorities attempted to keep the eager American settlers out of the Mesilla Valley, and the possibility of an armed clash continued. But in November, 1854, United States troops entered Mesilla, ending the controversy.

The official boundary survey was completed in 1856. By 1858 the first transcontinental stage line was running through the region, and in 1862, Congress had sanctioned the proposal for the Pacific Railroad. Ultimately, the Southern Pacific was to follow a route through the territory acquired by Gadsden, thereby endorsing the judgment of those who foresaw this purchase area as an essential transcontinental railroad route.

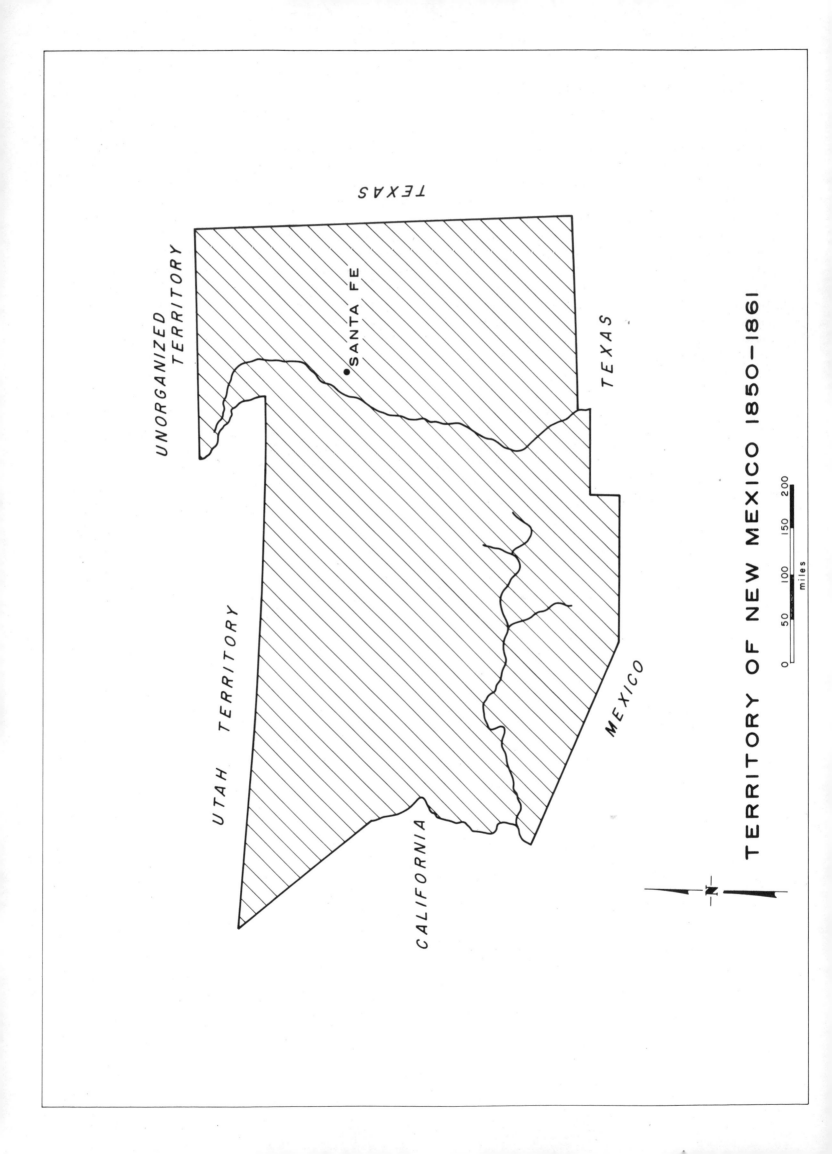

TERRITORY OF NEW MEXICO 1850–1861

TEXAS

UNORGANIZED TERRITORY

SANTA FE

TEXAS

UTAH TERRITORY

MEXICO

CALIFORNIA

0 50 100 150 200
miles

N

29. TERRITORY OF NEW MEXICO, 1850–1861

FROM 1850 TO 1861 the territory of New Mexico included the vast area comprising the present states of New Mexico and Arizona, with smaller portions of Colorado and Nevada. In 1853 the territory was farther expanded by addition of the area included in the Gadsden Purchase.

New Mexico barely missed statehood in 1850, going so far as to draft a constitution and hold state elections. The untimely death of President Zachary Taylor probably thwarted the bid for statehood, in spite of a population of 60,000. If this effort had been successful, the history of New Mexico would certainly have been different. Instead, territorial status was conferred as part of the Compromise of 1850; it was to be sixty years before statehood was granted.

During the decade of the 1850's, Anglo settlers moved into Arizona, enticed mainly by mining prospects. The slow but steady increase in population in the western portion of the territory called attention to the great difficulty of governing such a vast area. The necessity of traveling from Yuma to Santa Fe to conduct essential business provided an excuse for a territorial division. Then, too, the supposed difference between the Anglo settlers in Arizona and the predominantly Hispanic ones along the Río Grande provided another reason.

WYOMING

Lat. 42°

COLORADO

Arkansas River

KANSAS

Long. 100°

AREA

OKLAHOMA

NEW MEXICO

CLAIMED

BY

TEXAS

TEXAS
1836
TO
1845

Rio

Grande

N

THE TEXAS CLAIM

0   100   200   300   400

miles

30. THE TEXAS CLAIM AFTER THE CONCLUSION OF PEACE WITH MEXICO

TEXAS LAID CLAIM to all of the territory east of the Río Grande and then north from its source to the 42° line. This would have extended Texas' claims to 42° North Latitude and then southward along the line laid out by the Adams-Onís Treaty of 1819. The Lone Star State had long cast covetous eyes in the direction of Santa Fe. In 1841 it had attempted by means of the ill-fated Texan–Santa Fe Expedition to assert its claim.

The legality of the Texas claim rested on the Treaty of Velasco, which had been granted by the Mexican president, Antonio López de Santa Anna, after his defeat at the Battle of San Jacinto in 1836. Mexico had repudiated these claims on the grounds that the treaty had been obtained under duress. To many Texans, however, the Mexican War was really a fight to assert Texas claims to the Río Grande River. Confirmation of the Texas claim would have meant the inclusion of Santa Fe within Texas. Since this had been the capital of the province under the Spanish colonial governors long before Texas was settled, the claim seemed preposterous to many.

The effective governmental control of the Spaniards went as far east in colonial times as the hostile Indians would permit, and varied accordingly. Only infrequently did the claim extend into the eastern plains region. But it most certainly included the various small settlements scattered along the Canadian River and, in some instances, the tributaries of the Pecos. Some Texans recognized that their claims were at best tenuous and suggested that the Pecos might be a better western boundary for their state.

However, this more reasonable claim was rejected by the Texas Legislature, and by popular demand the claim to the Río Grande was pushed.

After a period in which Texas threatened the national government with force in a vain effort to enforce its claim to the disputed territory, the whole question was resolved as a part of the Compromise of 1850. The extreme Texas claims were rejected, and reasonable boundaries were established. Perhaps the most effective balm for the wounds of the Lone Star State was a compensation of $10,000,000. Unfortunately, boundary claims were to remain. In the El Paso area the fact that the Río Grande shifted its channel led to a long-drawn-out dispute that was not finally resolved until 1930.

Although the settlement established the eastern boundary at the 103rd meridian, many years were to elapse before the exact limits were established. In the subsequent laying out of the boundary, surveys were made both from the northern tip of the state and the southern. This left a gap of 130 miles between the two surveys. When the survey was completed, it was found the two lines did not meet; and since much time had passed since the previous survey, it was not possible to make adjustments, for many people were already settled in the area. Hence, a diagonal line was drawn arbitrarily to establish the state boundary. Congress had approved this line in 1891, and New Mexico discovered that it was one-half mile west of the 103rd meridian, which meant that a sizable section of the Mexican territory still found its way into the hands of Texans.

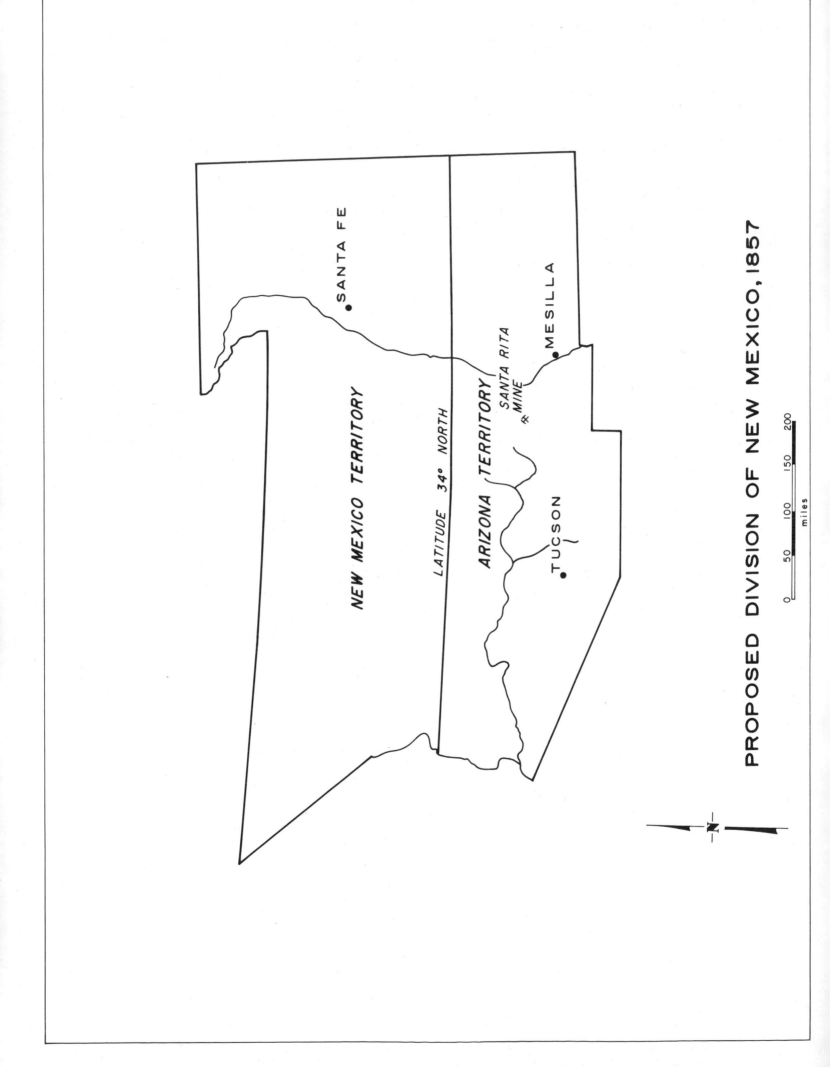

SANTA FE

NEW MEXICO TERRITORY

LATITUDE 34° NORTH

ARIZONA TERRITORY

SANTA RITA MINE

MESILLA

TUCSON

PROPOSED DIVISION OF NEW MEXICO, 1857

0   50   100   150   200
miles

N

31. PROPOSED DIVISION OF NEW MEXICO, 1857

THE TERRITORY OF NEW MEXICO established by the Compromise of 1850 was vastly greater in size than the present state. It originally included all of the present state of Arizona and portions of the states of Colorado and Nevada.

Arizona tried to separate from New Mexico before the Civil War several times. It was a long way from Arizona to Santa Fe, where people in the territory had to go to transact essential business. Also, there was friction between the Anglo settlements in Arizona and the predominantly Hispanic ones in New Mexico. Petitions asking Congress to authorize the formation of Arizona as a separate territory were drafted by meetings held in Tucson in 1857 and 1860. The latter petition proposed dividing the entire territory at the 33° 40′ line North Latitude, the southern portion to be designated Arizona, and the northern, New Mexico.

In 1857, and again a year later, President James Buchanan recommended to Congress that a territorial government for Arizona be created. Necessary legislation was introduced into Congress several times from 1857 to 1860 to no avail. Even the territorial legislature of New Mexico passed a resolution favoring a division, with a north-south boundary along the 109th meridian.

The national Congress being unable to act because of the sectional controversy, action of another kind was taken in March, 1861. At that time a Secessionist Convention at Mesilla declared Arizona to be a territory of the Confederacy. Following the defeat of the Union forces in July, 1861, Lieutenant Colonel John R. Baylor recognized the provisional territory of Arizona. (It was destined to be the only such territory of the Confederacy.) This was to embrace all of the existing territory of New Mexico south of the 34th parallel and have Mesilla as its capital. An independent convention held at Tucson took similar action, but when the Confederate Congress acted in January, 1862, the capital was set at Mesilla. The success of Union arms in 1862, however, doomed the only Confederate territory.

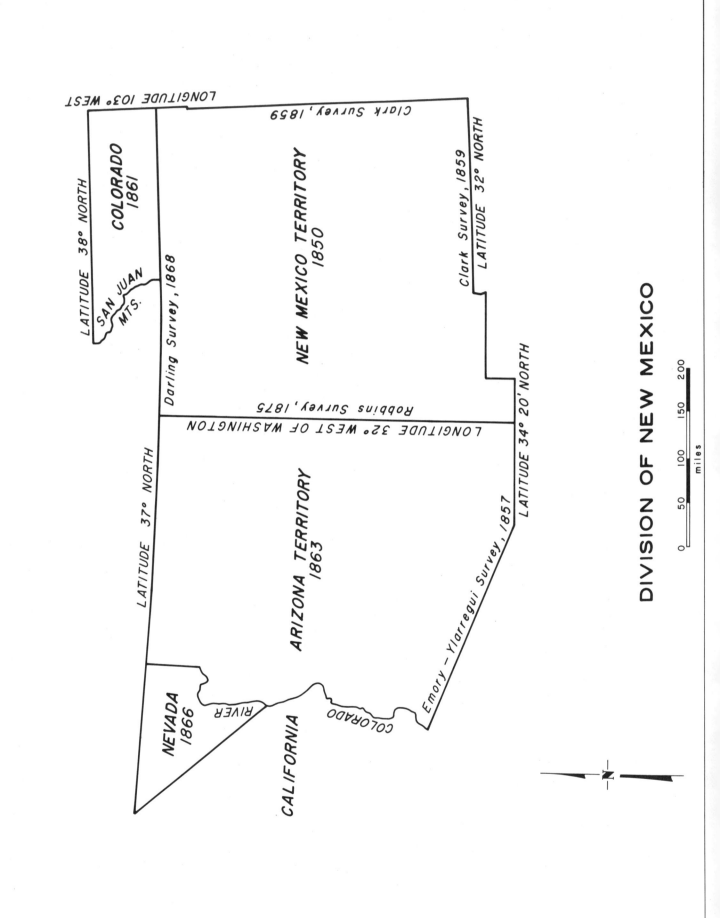

DIVISION OF NEW MEXICO

LONGITUDE 103° WEST

COLORADO
1861

LATITUDE 38° NORTH

SAN JUAN
MTS.

Clark Survey, 1859

NEW MEXICO TERRITORY
1850

Clark Survey, 1859

LATITUDE 32° NORTH

Darling Survey, 1868

Robbins Survey, 1875

LONGITUDE 32° WEST OF WASHINGTON

LATITUDE 34° 20' NORTH

LATITUDE 37° NORTH

ARIZONA TERRITORY
1863

Emory - Ylarregui Survey, 1857

NEVADA
1866

RIVER

CALIFORNIA

COLORADO

0   50   100   150   200
miles

N

32. DIVISION OF NEW MEXICO

THE ADVENT OF CIVIL WAR removed the issue of slavery in the territories and made it possible to get measures dealing with New Mexico's boundaries through Congress. In addition, Confederate military activity in the territory in 1861 made Washington authorities conscious of the area. Hence, the Arizona Territory bill was introduced into Congress in December, 1861, but with the press of more urgent matters was not signed into law until February, 1863. This measure fulfilled the desires of the Arizonans, and the new territory was created from the western half of New Mexico along the 32nd meridian (west of Washington, D.C.). The exact boundary line with Arizona was fixed by the Robbins Survey in 1875. In May, 1866, the north-western corner of Arizona was given to the recently admitted state of Nevada. In 1861 the area east of the San Juan Mountains and north of 37° North Latitude was shifted to the territory of Colorado. Although the Darling Survey of 1868 marked out the boundary with Colorado, the exact line was not established until 1960. The Clark Survey in 1859 set the southern boundary with Texas as well as the eastern boundary with that state. Unfortunately, the surveys of the eastern boundary were made from both north and south, and, as many years elapsed before their completion, the error was not discovered until after the area was settled. This made it possible for Texas to deprive New Mexico of approximately one-half-million acres of land.

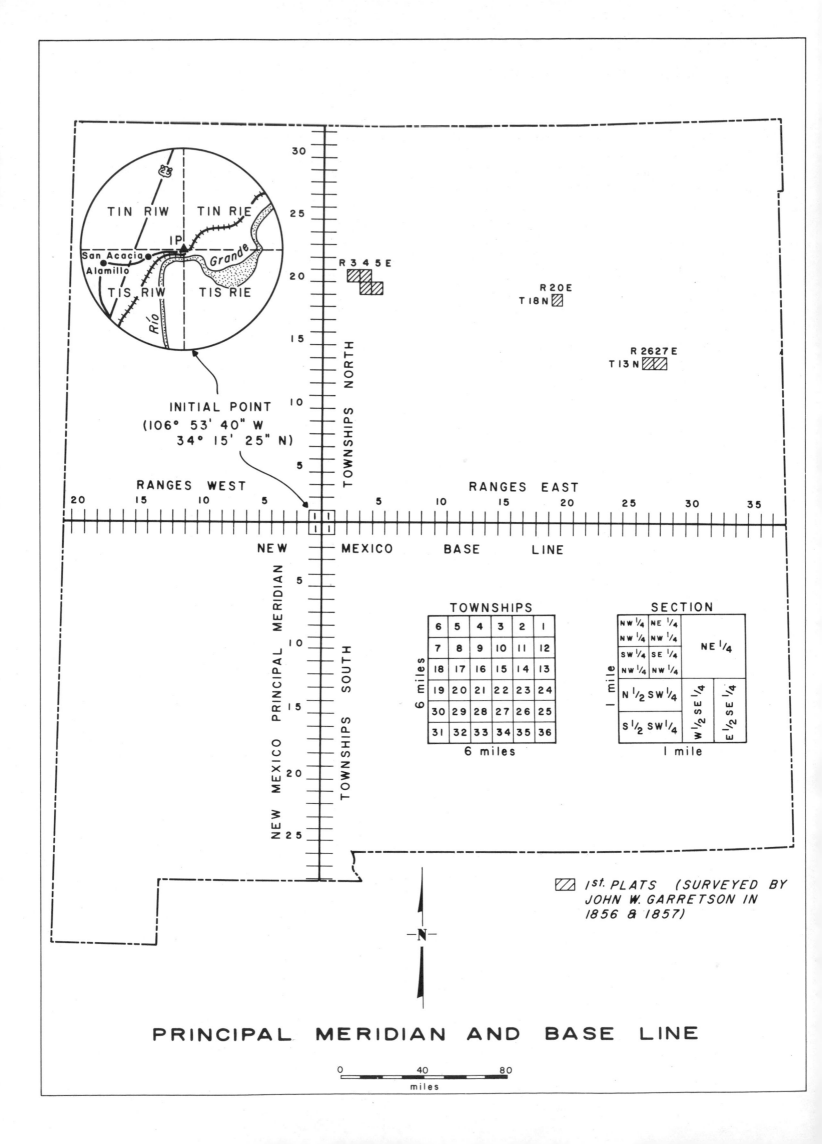

TIN RIW   TIN RIE

San Acacia
Alamillo

TIS RIW   TIS RIE

Río

Grande

IP

INITIAL POINT
(106° 53' 40" W
34° 15' 25" N)

30

25

20

15

10

5

TOWNSHIPS NORTH

RANGES WEST

20   15   10   5

RANGES EAST

5   10   15   20   25   30   35

R 3 4 5 E

R 20 E
T 18 N

R 2627 E
T 13 N

NEW   MEXICO   BASE   LINE

NEW MEXICO PRINCIPAL MERIDIAN

5

10

15

20

25

TOWNSHIPS SOUTH

TOWNSHIPS

6	5	4	3	2	1
7	8	9	10	11	12
18	17	16	15	14	13
19	20	21	22	23	24
30	29	28	27	26	25
31	32	33	34	35	36

6 miles

6 miles

SECTION

NW¼ NE¼		
NW¼ NW¼	NE¼	
SW¼ SE¼		
NW¼ NW¼		
N½ SW¼	W½ SE¼	E½ SE¼
S½ SW¼		

1 mile

1 mile

[hatch] 1ST. PLATS (SURVEYED BY
JOHN W. GARRETSON IN
1856 & 1857)

—N—

PRINCIPAL   MERIDIAN   AND   BASE   LINE

0   40   80
miles

THE UNITED STATES ADOPTED the rectangular system of public land surveys in 1785. The system was based on the manner in which old town grants had been made in early Massachusetts. The new rectangular plan was intended to make settlers take all of the land instead of the choice parcels only, to provide an orderly method of recording land titles, and to describe titles in such a way that duplication would be avoided. When the United States acquired the Southwest in the Mexican Cession of 1848, it inherited a very confused system of land tenure, which was at its worst in New Mexico. In the two and one-half centuries of Hispanic occupation, land was acquired most informally. In fact, the Hispanic manner of granting land title was anything but an exact science. Many landholders did not even possess the legal documents required to prove their ownership. Others had titles which described their holdings in such vague fashion it was impossible to define boundaries. It was common to use streams, hills, rocks, or even trees to mark land division. Then too, frequent transfers of titles or subdivisions were not properly recorded.

Under the peace treaty with Mexico in 1848 the United States government assumed the responsibility for certifying land titles which had existed previous to that date. In order to determine the extent and legality of these holdings, both public and private, which had been acquired under Spanish and Mexican rule, a control point had to be established which would permit land surveys that would be meaningful under the surveying system of the United States.

This control point was established in April, 1855, by John W. Garretson. He fixed the Initial Point on an isolated hill on the west bank of the Río Grande not far from the Mexican village of La Joyita in Socorro County. From this point he ran the Principal Meridan of New Mexico south to the International boundary and north 96 miles. The Base Line was run 21.5 miles west and 24 miles east of the Initial Point. A Guide Meridian and five Correction Lines were then run out. After this, an orderly program of cadastral or property boundary surveys were made. Most of the early township surveys were made on grant lands in an effort to help establish proper title. Unfortunately, the court operated much more slowly than did the surveyors, and it took years in many cases to prove legal ownership.

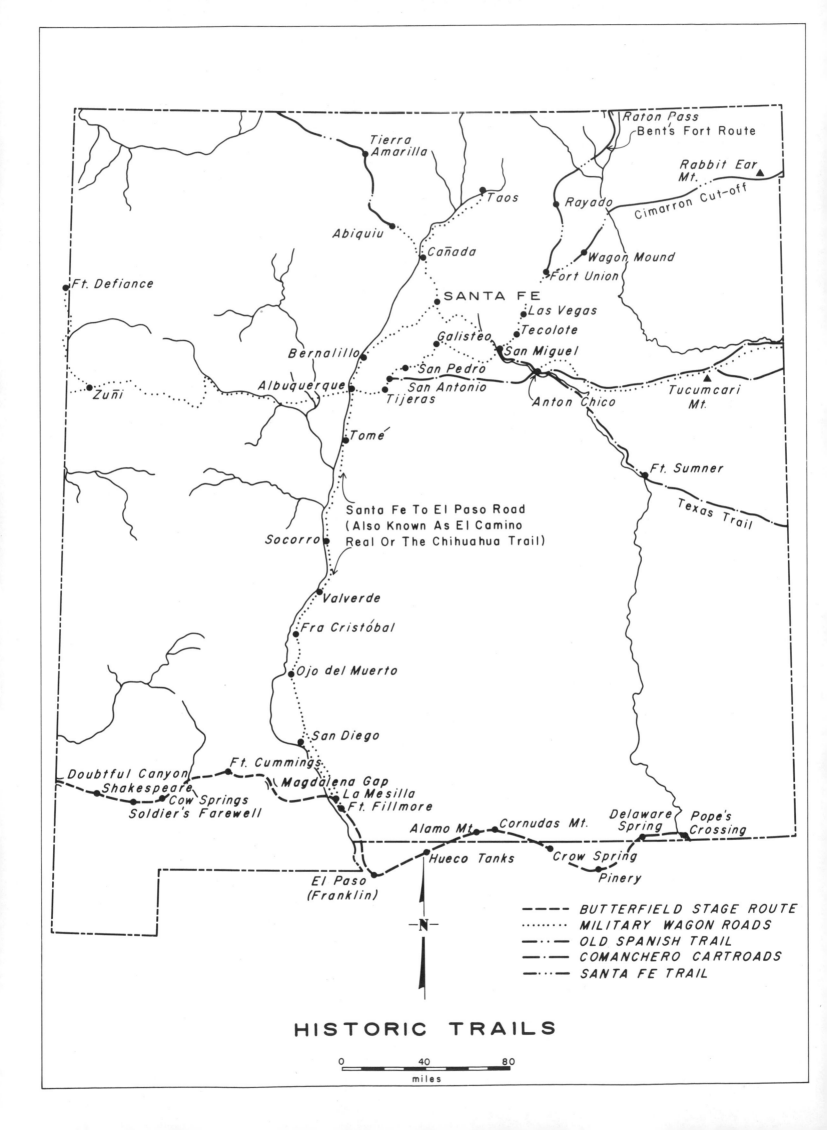

Tierra
Amarilla

Raton Pass
Bent's Fort Route

Rabbit Ear
Mt.

Taos

Rayado

Cimarron Cut-off

Abiquiu

Cañada

Wagon Mound

Fort Union

Ft. Defiance

SANTA FE

Las Vegas

Tecolote

Galisteo

San Miguel

Bernalillo

San Pedro

San Antonio

Zuñi

Albuquerque

Tijeras

Anton Chico

Tucumcari
Mt.

Tomé

Ft. Sumner

Texas Trail

Santa Fe To El Paso Road
(Also Known As El Camino
Real Or The Chihuahua Trail)

Socorro

Valverde

Fra Cristóbal

Ojo del Muerto

San Diego

Ft. Cummings

Doubtful Canyon

Shakespeare

Magdalena Gap

La Mesilla

Cow Springs

Ft. Fillmore

Soldier's Farewell

Delaware
Spring

Pope's
Crossing

Alamo Mt.

Cornudas Mt.

Hueco Tanks

Crow Spring

El Paso
(Franklin)

Pinery

—N—

BUTTERFIELD STAGE ROUTE

MILITARY WAGON ROADS

OLD SPANISH TRAIL

COMANCHERO CARTROADS

SANTA FE TRAIL

HISTORIC TRAILS

0   40   80

miles

Most important of the historic trails through New Mexico was the Santa Fe route over which the trade caravans came from Missouri. The Cimarron "cut-off" was extensively used in the early history of the trail in spite of the fifty-eight-mile journey from the Arkansas River to the Cimarron without water. The branch via Bent's Fort and Raton Pass was made hazardous by the mountain terrain but came to be preferred after Uncle Dick Wootton opened an improved toll road. The Santa Fe Trail remained the leading avenue of transit into New Mexico and was the route followed by the first railroad into the territory.

El Camino Real, or the Chihuahua Trail, developed as a natural outgrowth of travel between Santa Fe and Mexican cities to the south. In Spanish colonial times it was the route by which the Franciscan missions were supplied. Settlers made their way into New Mexico along it, and government officials or dispatch riders traversed it. Once trade over the Santa Fe trail became significant, a sizable percentage of United States consumer goods was shipped into Mexico via the Chihuahua Trail.

Unique among the historic trails were the Comanchero cart roads across the virtually treeless and waterless windswept plains of the Llano Estacado, which made this area a most difficult region for Anglo travelers or settlers. However, native New Mexicans known as Comancheros carried on an extensive trade with the Comanches, beginning in the eighteenth century.

Although it lasted for only a few years, the Butterfield stage route through New Mexico was one of the most famous roads. Stagecoach service began in 1858 and covered almost the width of the southern part of the territory. The route remained a significant link in transcontinental travel. The southwestern portion of the state was Apache country, so the route has figured prominently in New Mexican history.

To supply the many military installations that were established to control the Indians, the United States Army charted many wagon roads connecting the forts with the more settled population centers. Since these roads usually were planned to utilize natural passes through the mountains or across streams, they were used by the settlers and traders. Later they were flanked by railroad lines, and still later, by modern highways.

When missions were built in California in 1769, the hazards of the sea journey from Mexico provided an impetus to develop overland communications from New Mexico. This led to establishment of the Spanish Trail, a route initiated by those seeking mineral wealth in the area north of New Mexico. As early as 1765 an expedition under the leadership of Juan María de Rivera penetrated what is now Colorado and Utah. In the latter part of the eighteenth century, Spanish slave hunting expeditions brought back information about what had been a relatively unknown region. In 1776, Fathers Sylvestre Veles de Escalante and Francisco Atanasio Dominquez attempted to chart the trail to California. Although they failed, their efforts made possible the ultimate use of the Spanish Trail.

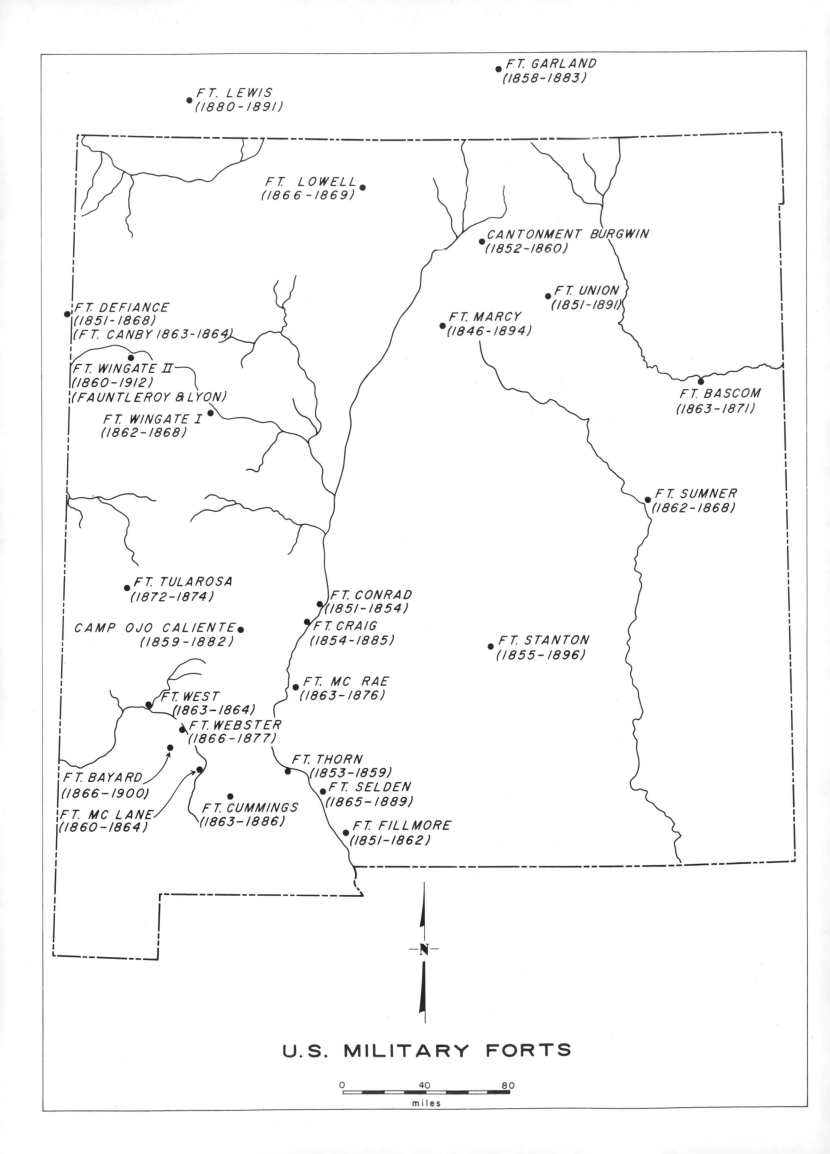

FT. GARLAND
(1858-1883)

FT. LEWIS
(1880-1891)

FT. LOWELL
(1866-1869)

CANTONMENT BURGWIN
(1852-1860)

FT. UNION
(1851-1891)

FT. DEFIANCE
(1851-1868)
(FT. CANBY 1863-1864)

FT. MARCY
(1846-1894)

FT. WINGATE II
(1860-1912)
(FAUNTLEROY & LYON)

FT. BASCOM
(1863-1871)

FT. WINGATE I
(1862-1868)

FT. SUMNER
(1862-1868)

FT. TULAROSA
(1872-1874)

FT. CONRAD
(1851-1854)

CAMP OJO CALIENTE
(1859-1882)

FT. CRAIG
(1854-1885)

FT. STANTON
(1855-1896)

FT. MC RAE
(1863-1876)

FT. WEST
(1863-1864)

FT. WEBSTER
(1866-1877)

FT. THORN
(1853-1859)

FT. BAYARD
(1866-1900)

FT. SELDEN
(1865-1889)

FT. MC LANE
(1860-1864)

FT. CUMMINGS
(1863-1886)

FT. FILLMORE
(1851-1862)

—N—

U.S. MILITARY FORTS

0   40   80

miles

ACQUISITION OF THE TERRITORY of New Mexico after the Mexican War made the United States responsible for protecting the area against hostile Indians. It was necessary to station troops in Indian country, and for these a large number of military posts were built. Many of these posts existed for only a short time to fill an immediate need. When the emergency had passed, they were abandoned as their garrisons moved elsewhere.

Fort Marcy, the first military post in the territory, was built by General Stephen Watts Kearny in 1846 at Santa Fe to protect the frontier settlements. Fort Union was established in 1851. Originally intended to be the supply base for other military installations, its primary duty became protection of traffic on the Santa Fe Trail. It remained the most important post in New Mexico until it was abandoned in 1891. To protect settlers from depredations by the Utes and the Jicarilla Apaches, Cantonment Burgwin (also referred to as Fort Fernando de Taos) was established in 1852, and Fort Lowell in 1866. Although outside the present boundaries of the state of New Mexico, Fort Lewis (1880), Fort Massachusetts (1852), and Fort Garland (1858) were within the territory and military department, and also served to check the Utes and the Jicarillas.

In an effort to control the Navahos better, the army built three forts in their country. Fort Defiance was established in 1851 (known briefly as Fort Canby, 1863–64). Fort Wingate II was originally commissioned as Fort Fauntleroy in 1860 but was renamed Fort Lyon in 1861 when General Fauntleroy defected to the Confederacy. Fort Wingate I was established in 1862 but abandoned in 1868, the garrison and name being transferred to Fort Wingate II. Although the army left in 1912, the post remains as Fort Wingate Ordnance Depot.

To control the many tribes of Apaches in the southwestern part of the state, to protect the travelers en route to California, and to make possible the working of copper, silver, and gold deposits in the area, several forts were established. Fort McLane (also referred to as Fort Floyd, Camp Webster, and Fort Webster) was established in 1860 and abandoned in 1864. Located to protect the Mesilla-Tucson Road, Fort Cummings played a noteworthy role in the campaigns against the Apaches. Fort Bayard near Silver City was also strategic in the long conflict with the Apaches. Of lesser significance were Camp Ojo Caliente, Fort Tularosa, Fort West, and Fort Webster. The last named fort had four locations.

To protect the main line of march along the Río Grande, a number of forts were erected. Most important of these were Fort Craig (1854), and Fort Selden (1865), and Fort Fillmore (1851). The latter fort combined with near-by Fort Bliss (Texas) to protect the southern route to California. Lesser forts were Conrad, McRae, and Thorn. Fort Stanton had the difficult task of containing the Sacramento and White Mountain Mescalero Apaches from 1855 to 1896. Fort Sumner was located at Bosque Redondo to guard this area while the Navahos were in reluctant residence. Fort Bascom was established to guard the travel routes across central New Mexico, to discourage incursions by the Kiowa Apaches and the Comanches, and to protect settlements along the Canadian River.

Most of these forts were poorly garrisoned, and the infantry had little success chasing mounted Indians. The cavalry force was too small to do more than chastise those Indians who violated the peace. With all of their deficiencies, the forts of New Mexico ultimately were able to combat the Indian menace, to help create a transportation system of supply lines, and to provide a means whereby the United States could learn about the vast area of the Southwest which it had acquired from Mexico.

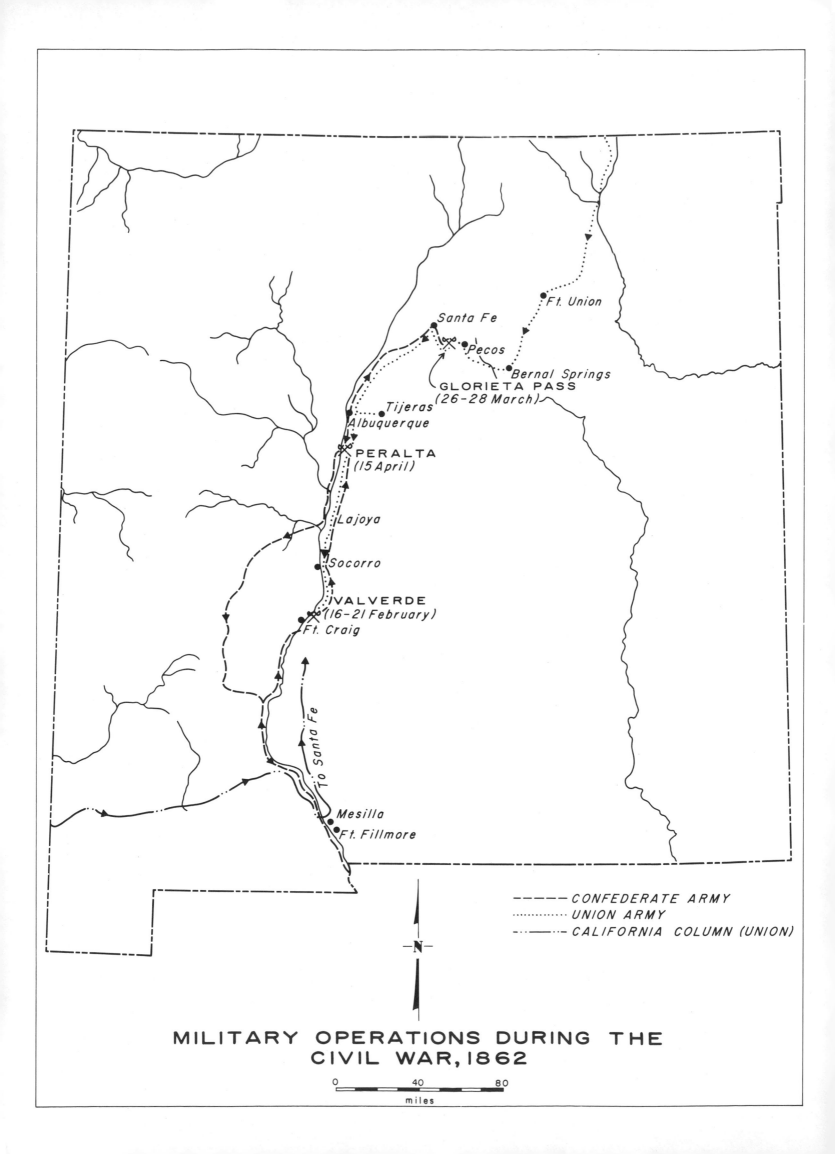

Ft. Union

Santa Fe

Pecos

Bernal Springs

GLORIETA PASS
(26-28 March)

Tijeras
Albuquerque

PERALTA
(15 April)

Lajoya

Socorro

VALVERDE
(16-21 February)

Ft. Craig

To Santa Fe

Mesilla
Ft. Fillmore

—N—

- - - - — CONFEDERATE ARMY
· · · · · · · · UNION ARMY
—··—··— CALIFORNIA COLUMN (UNION)

MILITARY OPERATIONS DURING THE
CIVIL WAR, 1862

0   40   80

miles

WHEN THE WAR CAME TO NEW MEXICO in the summer of 1861, it appeared that the Confederate plan for conquering the Southwest was not just a wild dream, but one capable of realization. On July 1, 1861, Captain John Robert Baylor, in command of 258 Texas cavalry, occupied Fort Bliss. Later in the month Baylor moved his forces northward, occupying Mesilla, and, after very little resistance, took Fort Fillmore, capturing most of the Union troops stationed there. Baylor thereupon issued a proclamation in the name of the Confederate States of America establishing the territory of Arizona, with Mesilla as the capital.

After the debacle at Fort Fillmore, Colonel Canby, the United States military departmental commander, found his situation in New Mexico critical because of insufficient supplies. Recognizing that the Confederates must invade by one of two routes, either over the Santa Fe Trail or up the Río Grande, he prepared his defenses accordingly. To protect the heart of New Mexico, Canby abandoned all the forts except Fort Craig along the Río Grande, where he could check the Confederates coming up the river, and Fort Union, which would block entry from the east.

General Henry Sibley led a Confederate Army of approximately 3,700 men up the Río Grande. The first battle was fought February 16–21, 1862, at Valverde near Fort Craig. Canby's forces were compelled to flee. A loss of supplies, however, made it impossible for Sibley to lay siege to Fort Craig. Thus he had to leave the Union Army in the rear as he marched up the Río Grande.

Sibley made his triumphant way up the river, easily taking Albuquerque and Santa Fe, but capturing few of the supplies he sorely needed. News of the Confederate invasion had prompted the dispatch of 1,300 Colorado troops under the command of Colonel John P. Slough. The two forces met at Glorieta Pass March 26–28. Again, the Union troops, outnumbered, were forced to retire, but the destruction of supply wagons compelled the Confederates to retreat to Santa Fe and then down the river. Meanwhile, the Colorado troops joined with Colonel Canby's forces at Tijeras, and on the fifteenth of April fought an undecisive skirmish with the Confederates at Peralta. Very short of supplies, Sibley and the Confederate Army retreated southward, making a wide swing to the west to avoid Fort Craig and escape from New Mexico as quickly as possible.

Perhaps if Sibley had known that the North had organized a 5,000-man division at Fort Leavenworth to march to the aid of New Mexico, he would have left earlier. In addition, 1,500 men under the command of General Carleton made their way across the desert from California, arriving in New Mexico shortly after Sibley and his Texans had fled. Carleton's forces were to find no Confederates to contend with, but the Indians would more than keep them busy. Had the Confederates won control of New Mexico, the story of the Civil War might have been different, and far more significance would have been attached to the New Mexico campaign.

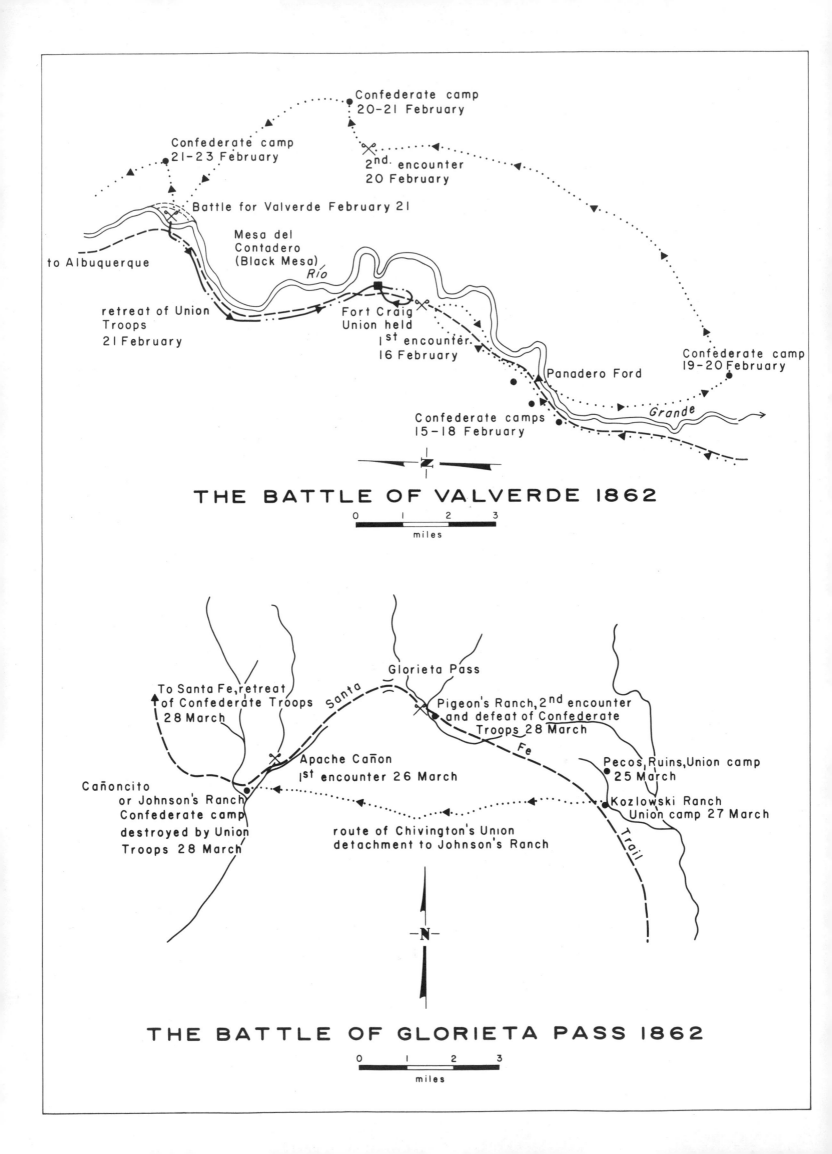

Confederate camp
20-21 February

2nd encounter
20 February

Confederate camp
21-23 February

Battle for Valverde February 21

Mesa del
Contadero
(Black Mesa)

to Albuquerque

Río

retreat of Union
Troops
21 February

Fort Craig
Union held
1st encounter
16 February

Confederate camp
19-20 February

Panadero Ford

Confederate camps
15-18 February

Grande

N

THE BATTLE OF VALVERDE 1862

0   1   2   3
miles

Glorieta Pass

To Santa Fe, retreat
of Confederate Troops
28 March

Santa

Pigeon's Ranch, 2nd encounter
and defeat of Confederate
Troops 28 March

Fe

Apache Cañon
1st encounter 26 March

Pecos Ruins, Union camp
25 March

Cañoncito
or Johnson's Ranch
Confederate camp
destroyed by Union
Troops 28 March

route of Chivington's Union
detachment to Johnson's Ranch

Kozlowski Ranch
Union camp 27 March

Trail

-N-

THE BATTLE OF GLORIETA PASS 1862

0   1   2   3
miles

37. THE BATTLE OF VALVERDE, 1862; THE BATTLE OF GLORIETA PASS, 1862

Two NOTEWORTHY BATTLES of the Civil War were fought in New Mexico. The Battle of Valverde, fought on February 21, 1862, was the first major conflict between Union and Confederate forces in the Intermountain West. This battle site is located about 3 miles east of United States Highway 85 and approximately 100 miles south of Albuquerque.

As General Sibley's Confederate Army moved up the Río Grande toward Santa Fe, it confronted General Canby's Union Army at Fort Craig. The first encounter took place on February 16 and convinced the Southern forces that they had to lure the Northern armies into the open if they were to win. To accomplish this, the Confederates crossed to the east bank of the river planning to locate their artillery on a hill in order to bombard the fort. The Union forces had anticipated this, however, and came into the open for the fight the Confederates were seeking. At a key moment in the battle, poorly trained local militia refused to cross the river and join the fighting. The Federal Army was therefore forced to retreat to Fort Craig. There were about 200 casualties on both sides, but the Battle of Valverde was clearly a Southern victory.

Glorieta Pass was one of the traditional routes of the American Southwest. Indians, Spaniards, and Anglo frontiersmen had appreciated its strategic importance, and it continues to be a major transportation route. The Texans fought a skirmish with Union forces on March 26, 1862, at the narrow western end called Apache Cañon. They fought the main battle two days later when the Confederates attacked. Because of the rugged terrain, much of the combat was hand to hand. Late in the afternoon the Union forces retreated to their camp at Kozlowski Ranch in another apparent defeat. However, while the major battle had raged, Major Chivington had led a detachment through the mountains to Cañoncito and was able to destroy almost all of the Confederates' ammunition, food, and horses. This turned an apparent setback into a major victory which made it impossible for the Confederate forces to remain in New Mexico.

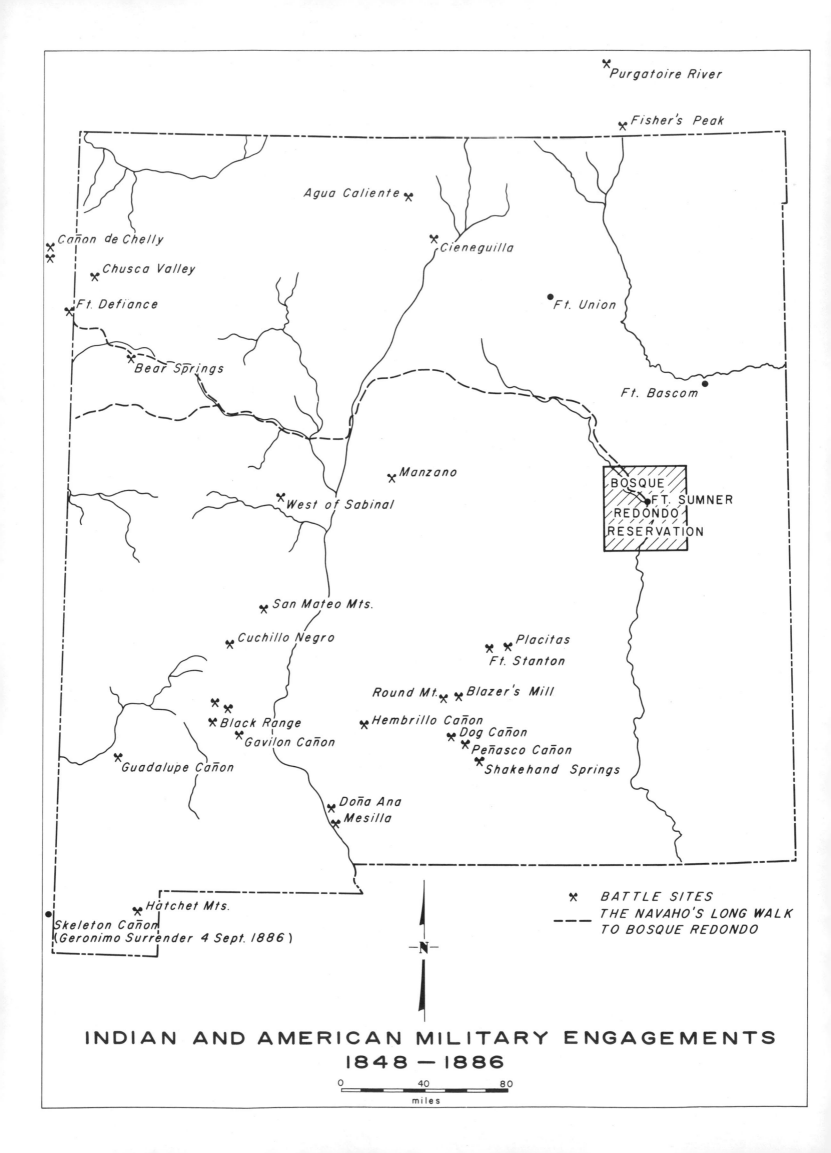

✗ *Purgatoire River*

✗ *Fisher's Peak*

✗ *Agua Caliente*

✗ *Cañon de Chelly*

✗ *Cieneguilla*

✗ *Chusca Valley*

● *Ft. Union*

✗ *Ft. Defiance*

✗ *Bear Springs*

● *Ft. Bascom*

✗ *Manzano*

✗ *West of Sabinal*

BOSQUE
● FT. SUMNER
REDONDO
RESERVATION

✗ *San Mateo Mts.*

✗ *Cuchillo Negro*

✗ *Placitas*
✗ *Ft. Stanton*

✗ *Round Mt.* ✗ *Blazer's Mill*

✗✗ *Black Range*
✗ *Gavilon Cañon*

✗ *Hembrillo Cañon*

✗ *Dog Cañon*
✗ *Peñasco Cañon*
✗ *Shakehand Springs*

✗ *Guadalupe Cañon*

✗ *Doña Ana*
✗ *Mesilla*

✗ *BATTLE SITES*
- - - *THE NAVAHO'S LONG WALK*
TO BOSQUE REDONDO

✗ *Hatchet Mts.*
● *Skeleton Cañon*
(Geronimo Surrender 4 Sept. 1886)

─ N ─

INDIAN AND AMERICAN MILITARY ENGAGEMENTS
1848 — 1886

0   40   80

miles

38. INDIAN AND AMERICAN MILITARY ENGAGEMENTS, 1848–1886

WHEN THE UNITED STATES acquired the Mexican Cession, it also acquired the responsibility for controlling the Indians in the area. To accomplish this, the United States built many forts, sent out a number of troops, and expended huge sums of money. The process of control was to take forty years.

Although General Kearny had received representatives of the Pueblos, Navahos, Utes, and Apaches, who surrendered in 1846, conflict was inevitable because the Indian's way of life was challenged by the white settler. To control the Indian more efficiently, New Mexico was made the Ninth Military Department, with headquarters at Fort Union.

The Navahos were first to challenge the Americans, and the 1850's were a period of almost constant conflict. From their supposedly impregnable fortress of Cañon de Chelly, they preyed upon the surrounding countryside. Although Fort Defiance was established to control them, it was not until Colonel Kit Carson defeated them and forced them to take their "long walk" to Bosque Redondo that the Navaho menace was removed.

The Mescalero Apaches were on the warpath about the same time as the Navahos and were also herded to Bosque Redondo, only to flee in 1865. Fort Stanton was the center from which this tribe was ultimately controlled. However, it was the Chiricahua Apaches in western New Mexico that were to prove most troublesome. Roaming over much of Arizona, northern Mexico, and the southwestern corner of New Mexico, they were on the warpath almost continuously from 1862, under the leadership of Cochise and Mangas Coloradas, until Geronimo was captured in 1886.

The Jicarilla Apaches made northeastern New Mexico their home grounds and also roamed into Colorado with the Utes, frequently their allies. Conflict resulted in 1852 when a raiding party attacked a wagon train, killing several people and taking others captive. Several engagements were fought in the next two years; but it was not until a force of regular troops—combined with Pueblo Indian allies and led by the famed Kit Carson—chased the Indians into the mountains, that they were defeated. In an effort to control these tribes, Cantonment Burgwin (1852) and Fort Massachusetts (1852), the latter abandoned and replaced by Fort Garland in 1858, were established. The fact that the Utes and the Jicarillas were loyal to the Union during the Civil War showed how effectively they had been chastised.

Although the Comanches belonged to the entire southern plains area and not to New Mexico alone, they invaded settlements in that state as early as the eighteenth century. Later they attacked travelers along the Santa Fe Trail and the Navahos at Bosque Redondo. Fort Bascom was established for the specific purpose of containing these fierce Plains Indians, but it was not until 1874 that a winter campaign launched from Forts Union, Bascom, and Sumner defeated the Comanches east of New Mexico and made the Llano Estacado safe for settlers.

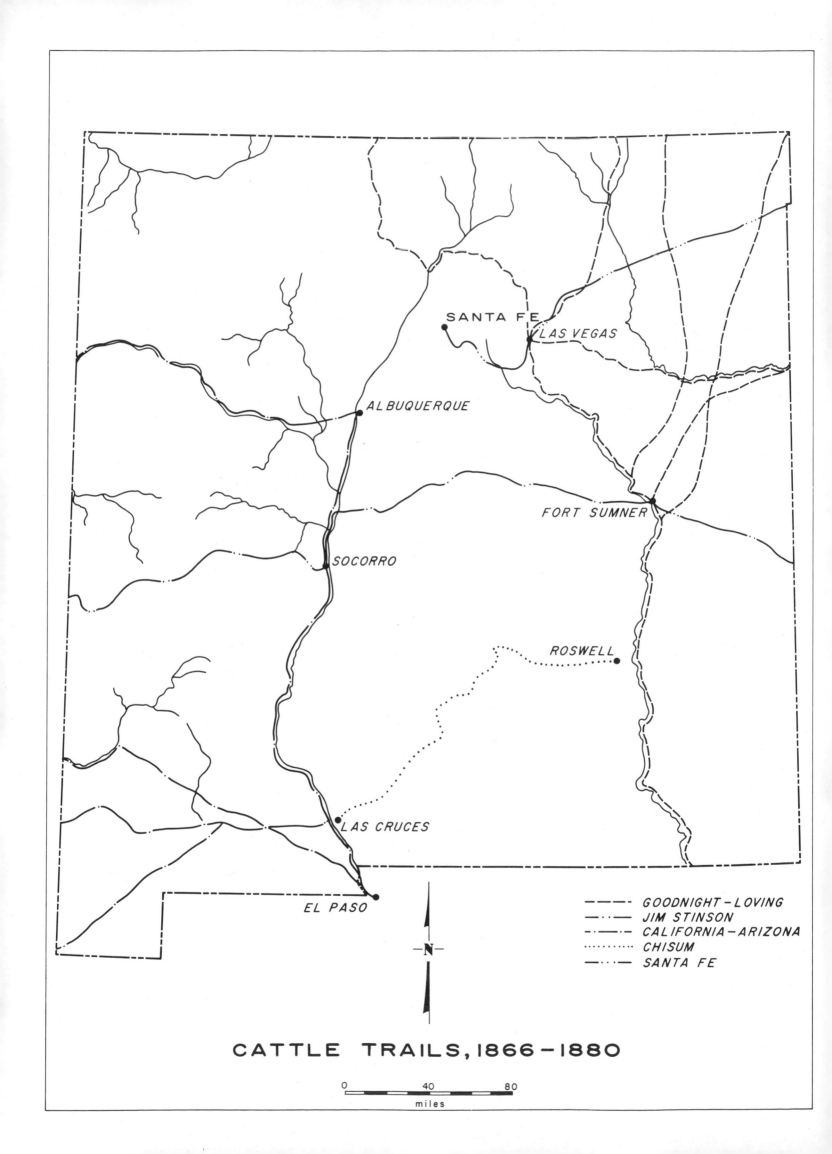

SANTA FE

LAS VEGAS

ALBUQUERQUE

FORT SUMNER

SOCORRO

ROSWELL

LAS CRUCES

EL PASO

-N-

— — — GOODNIGHT-LOVING
— ·— ·— JIM STINSON
— · — · — CALIFORNIA-ARIZONA
· · · · · · · CHISUM
— ·· — ·· — SANTA FE

CATTLE TRAILS, 1866-1880

0   40   80
miles

39. CATTLE TRAILS, 1866–1880

OÑATE HAD INTRODUCED CATTLE into New Mexico in 1598, but they never assumed a large commercial role until after the Civil War. Sheep were much more suited to the needs of those who lived in New Mexico before the Anglos became numerous.

Cattle had been driven into the area as early as 1847, but because of large numbers of cattle in downstate Texas and inflated beef prices in the post–Civil War period, the great cattle drives did not begin until 1866. Instead of heading herds toward the terminus of the railroads, Charles Goodnight and Oliver Loving drove their cattle into New Mexico. Gold miners eagerly purchased the cattle. Goodnight and Loving also found a ready market at military posts; for in addition to meeting the needs of the soldiers, the government was obliged to feed Indians on the reservations.

Cattle were also driven north through New Mexico to feed miners in Colorado and to stock the range lands as far away as Montana. But many Texas cattlemen saw the potential in New Mexico and remained. By controlling the water supply, a rancher could lay claim to the vast land area over which his cattle grazed. The inadequacy of land titles in the Spanish-Mexican period soon made it possible for a few cattle barons to control much of the area of the territory. Thus, the stage was set for conflicts between ranchers, and later between cattlemen and those who sought to divide the area into small plots and farm it.

The early cattlemen of New Mexico faced countless problems. At first the worst of these were attacks by Indians, who were more often after horses than cattle. What cattle the Indians did steal were usually for trading rather than consumption. Wherever cattle have grazed, rustlers have hovered about to steal them. Since many of the new migrants into New Mexico had left home to evade legal prosecution, it was inevitable that cattle thievery should be extensive. Then, too, native New Mexicans were not morally opposed to rustling, especially if the owners were Texans. Many times, stolen cattle could be traced to the corrals of New Mexicans, but getting them back through the local courts was virtually impossible for the outsider; hence, Texans usually took the law into their own hands, practicing frontier justice on cattle thieves. This use of force increased enmity toward the outsiders.

Even without the hazards of preying Indians and rustlers, the early cattlemen had to contend with the elements. Years of drought that shriveled the grass and dried up the waterholes, caused many a rancher to go bankrupt. Fire was one of the worst dangers in the early days. Sometimes grass fires burned for weeks on end. Undue cold and heavy snows likewise did much damage during the winter.

By the end of the nineteenth century, cattle were raised in almost every part of the state. Large ranches, totaling perhaps thirty or forty square miles, dotted the eastern side of the state, extending northward to the Colorado line. Similar ranches also were to be found in the northwestern part of the state, and in today's cattle country around Magdalena. Barbed wire, nesters, and blooded stock gradually invaded and put an end to the open range, although in parts of New Mexico it still remains, a romantic reminder of the hectic past.

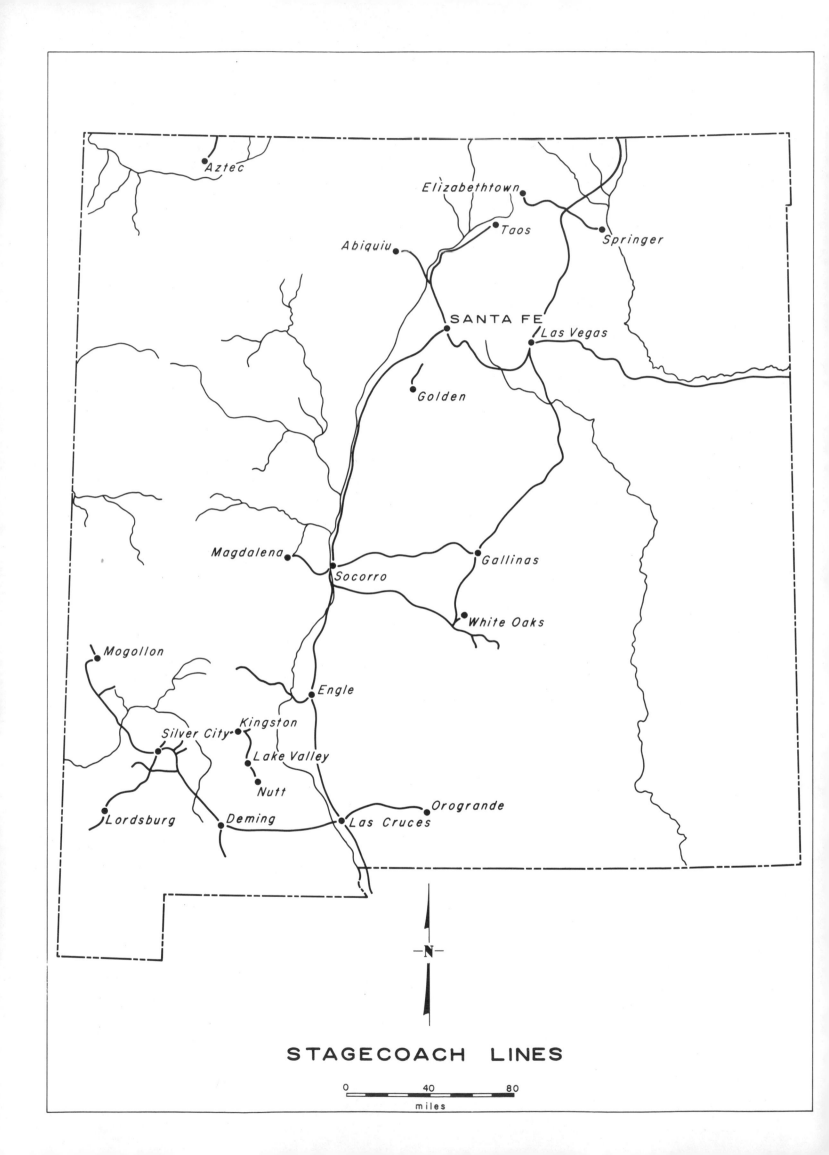

Aztec

Elizabethtown

Taos

Abiquiu

Springer

SANTA FE

Las Vegas

Golden

Magdalena

Gallinas

Socorro

White Oaks

Mogollon

Engle

Kingston

Silver City

Lake Valley

Nutt

Lordsburg

Deming

Las Cruces

Orogrande

—N—

STAGECOACH LINES

0   40   80
miles

40. STAGECOACH LINES

IN A VAST TERRITORY such as New Mexico which had no navigable rivers, it was inevitable that the stagecoach would be an important means of transportation as soon as the Anglos arrived. The stagecoach went through two periods of development. The first period was from 1849 to 1879 when the railroads were being built. During this era, stagecoaches were virtually the only form of public transportation. In the post-1879 period, stagecoaches were used as feeder lines to meet trains. They performed this function into the twentieth century, when they were succeeded by the motor coach.

The first stagecoach to enter New Mexico came from Independence, Missouri, to Santa Fe in 1849. Initially, the service was monthly, but it was later expanded so that stagecoaches arrived and departed every day. Fares were $250 one way. More than thirteen days were required to fill the schedule. Because national transportation lines, such as the Butterfield line, provided good east-west service across New Mexico, most of the state stagecoach lines ran north and south. By 1882 there were thirty-eight separate lines in New Mexico, the longest of these being the 90-mile-long Deming-Mogollon line.

In addition to the obvious function of carrying passengers for some 10.5 cents per mile, the stagecoaches sought mail contracts in order to show a profit. They also served as a most important way of shipping express packages on the frontier, in spite of the relatively high charges. It cost $18.00 per hundred pounds to ship a package from Pueblo, Colorado, to Las Vegas, for example. Finally, the stage lines laid out their route with an eye to serving the United States Army posts. Because of its own limited transportation system, the military placed great reliance on the commercial stage lines for communication between the various forts. Carrying service personnel, their dependents, and those doing business, not to mention essential freight, frequently made it possible for the stage lines to show a profit. Obviously other benefits accrued. Cavalry units provided much-needed protection at times, and even some military assisted in laying out the best stagecoach routes.

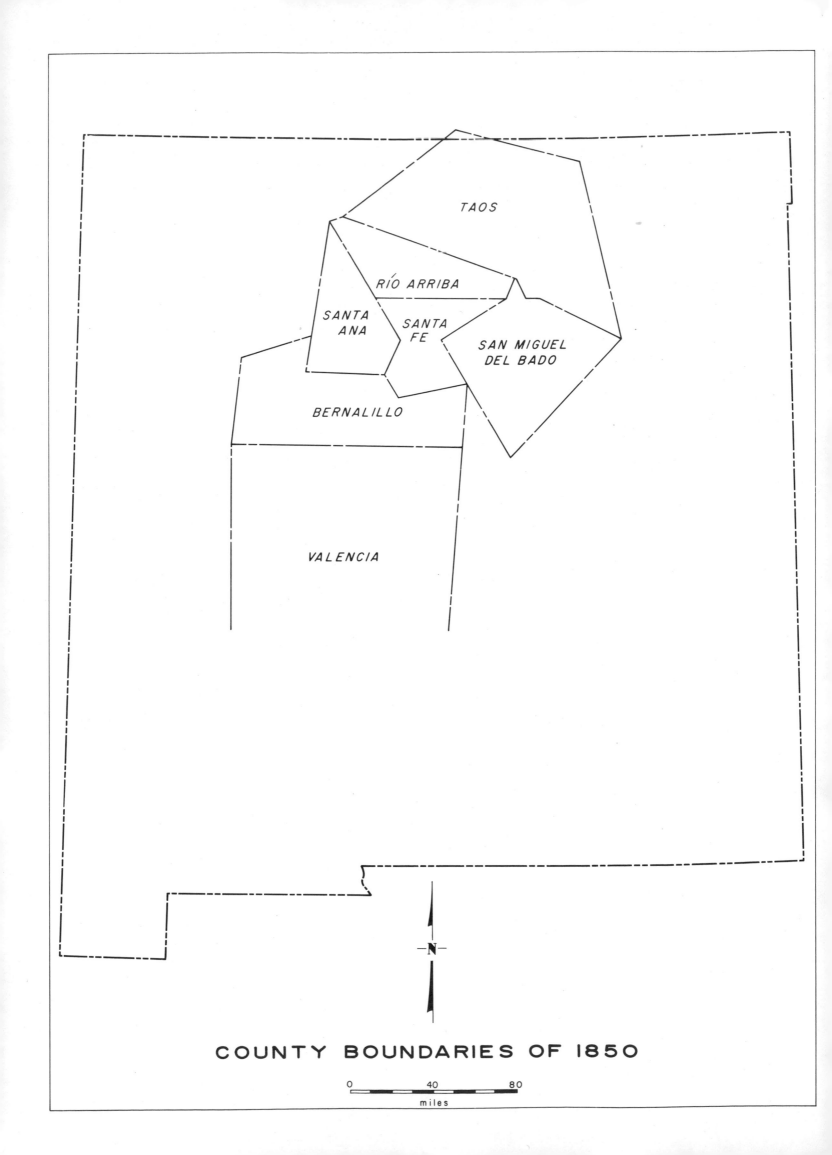

TAOS

RÍO ARRIBA

SANTA
ANA

SANTA
FE

SAN MIGUEL
DEL BADO

BERNALILLO

VALENCIA

N

COUNTY BOUNDARIES OF 1850

0   40   80
miles

41–42. COUNTY BOUNDARIES OF 1850 AND 1852

THE COUNTY BOUNDARIES of New Mexico have gone through no less than a dozen changes during the history of the state since it became a part of the United States. Although it was mistakenly assumed that the original county organization rested upon a Mexican division into counties, this is inaccurate. The area was divided into districts under Mexican rule. Three major districts had been created June 17, 1844. Each of these was under the political administration of a prefect, who was, in turn, directly responsible to the governor. The northern district covered the areas approximating the boundaries of Río Arriba, Taos, and Mora counties. The center district included Santa Fe and the surrounding area, as well as San Miguel County. The southeast was administered from Albuquerque, and included a vast area whose eastern boundaries were ill defined. It was designated the "southeast," since New Mexico at that time included all of the area east of the Colorado River.

The unusual shapes of the counties, established when New Mexico first became a territory in 1850, were altered in January, 1852, when the counties were laid out in an entirely different manner. With the exception of Santa Fe, San Miguel, Río Arriba, and Santa Ana, each one stretched from Texas to California. Doña Ana County was expanded in 1855 to include the territory purchased from Mexico in the Gadsden Purchase. Socorro County, which did not exist on the 1850 maps, was bounded on the west by the California line, on the east by the Texas line, and on the north by Valencia County. Exact boundaries are difficult to define because of the vast area embraced, lack of geographical knowledge of the region, and many changes in place names. Since most of the area was unpopulated, however, precise county lines were unnecessary.

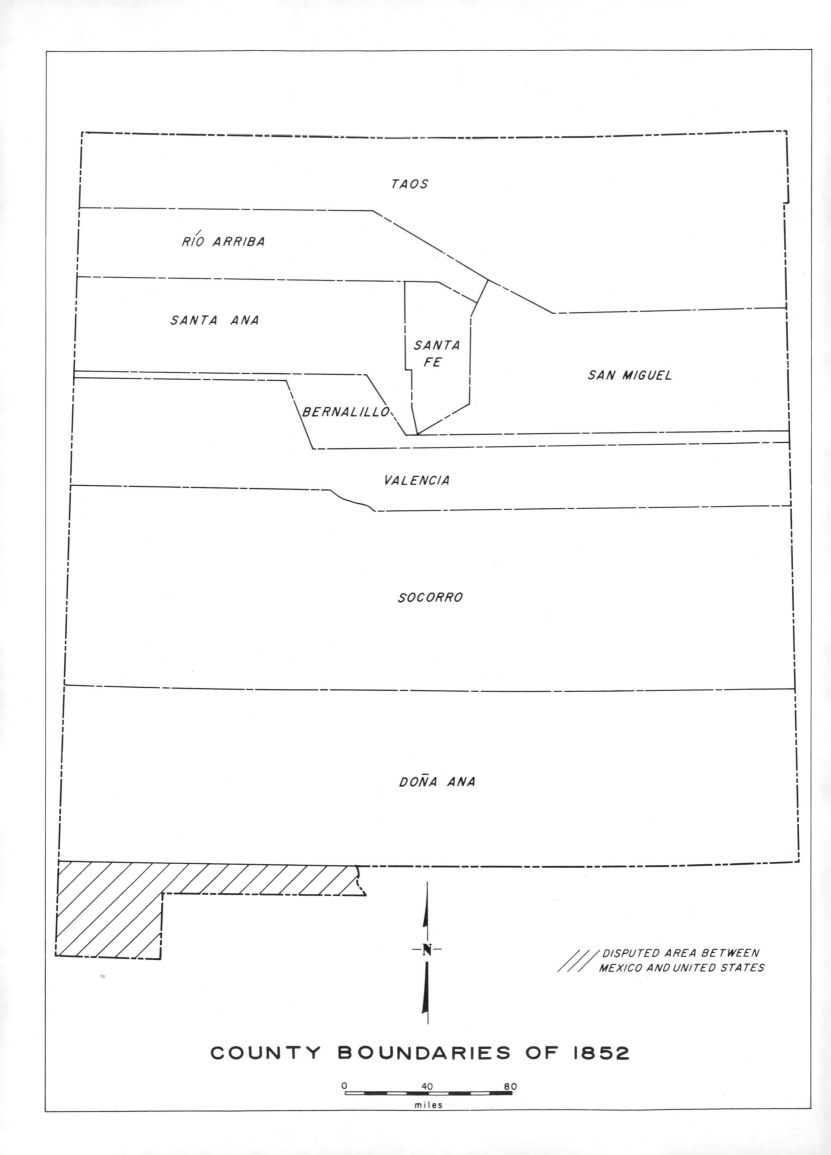

TAOS

RÍO ARRIBA

SANTA ANA

SANTA FE

SAN MIGUEL

BERNALILLO

VALENCIA

SOCORRO

DOÑA ANA

N

/// DISPUTED AREA BETWEEN
MEXICO AND UNITED STATES

COUNTY BOUNDARIES OF 1852

0   40   80

miles

42. COUNTY BOUNDARIES OF 1852

(A description of this map is included in the discussion on the preceding page.)

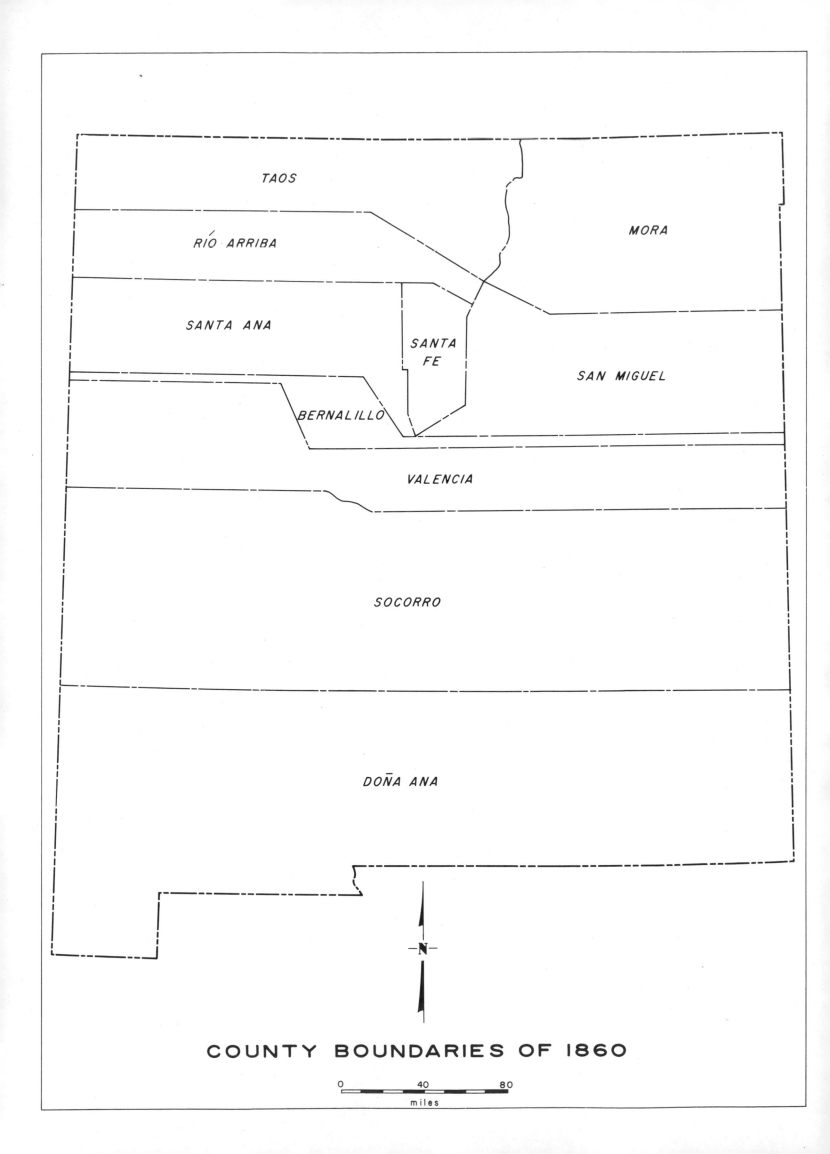

TAOS

RÍO ARRIBA

MORA

SANTA ANA

SANTA
FE

SAN MIGUEL

BERNALILLO

VALENCIA

SOCORRO

DOÑA ANA

N

COUNTY BOUNDARIES OF 1860

0   40   80
miles

43–44. COUNTY BOUNDARIES OF 1860 AND 1870

IN 1860 the territorial legislature created two new counties. One of these was Mora County, bounded on the north and east by the present New Mexico state line, on the south by San Miguel County, and on the west by the ridge that divides the Taos Valley from the valleys of Mora and Rayado. The other was Arizona County, which included all of that part of Doña Ana County west of the north-south line passing through a point one mile east of the overland mail station in Apache Canyon. San Juan County was created in 1861 in the northwest corner of the state, but the following year both Arizona and San Juan counties were eliminated, and in 1863, Congress created the territory of Arizona.

The eastern boundary of Santa Fe County was altered in 1864. The southern boundary of Socorro County was redefined in 1867. In 1868 the boundary between Taos and Mora counties was also altered somewhat. Grant County was created in the same year. It was bounded on the south by the Mexican line, on the west by the Arizona line, on the north by an east and west line running through Ojo del Muerto, and on the east by a line drawn north and south between Township Ranges Seven and Eight west.

Lincoln County was created in 1869 out of the eastern part of Socorro County. Colfax County was created out of Mora in 1869. It was bounded on the north by the Colorado line, on the east by the Texas line, on the south by the Rayado land grant, and on the west by Taos County. The southern boundary of Bernalillo County was slightly altered in 1870.

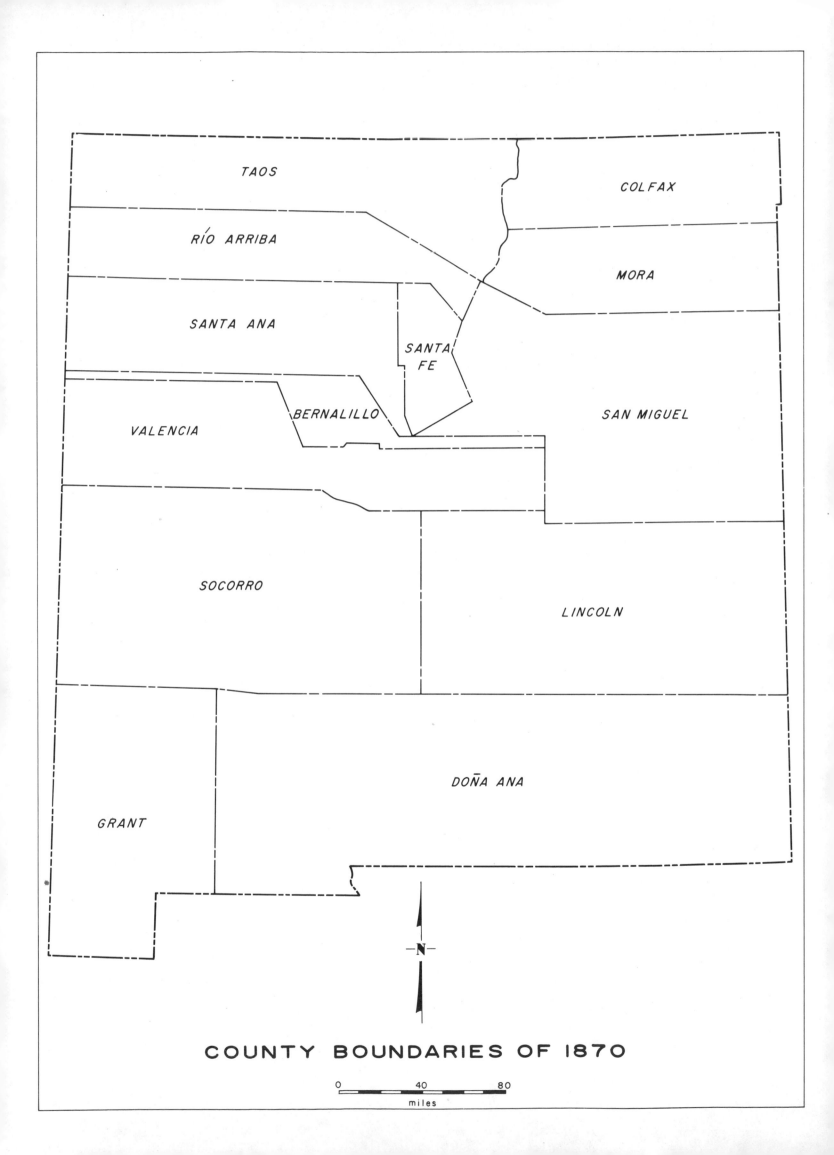

COUNTY BOUNDARIES OF 1870

0   40   80
miles

44. COUNTY BOUNDARIES OF 1870

(A description of this map is included in the discussion on the preceding page.)

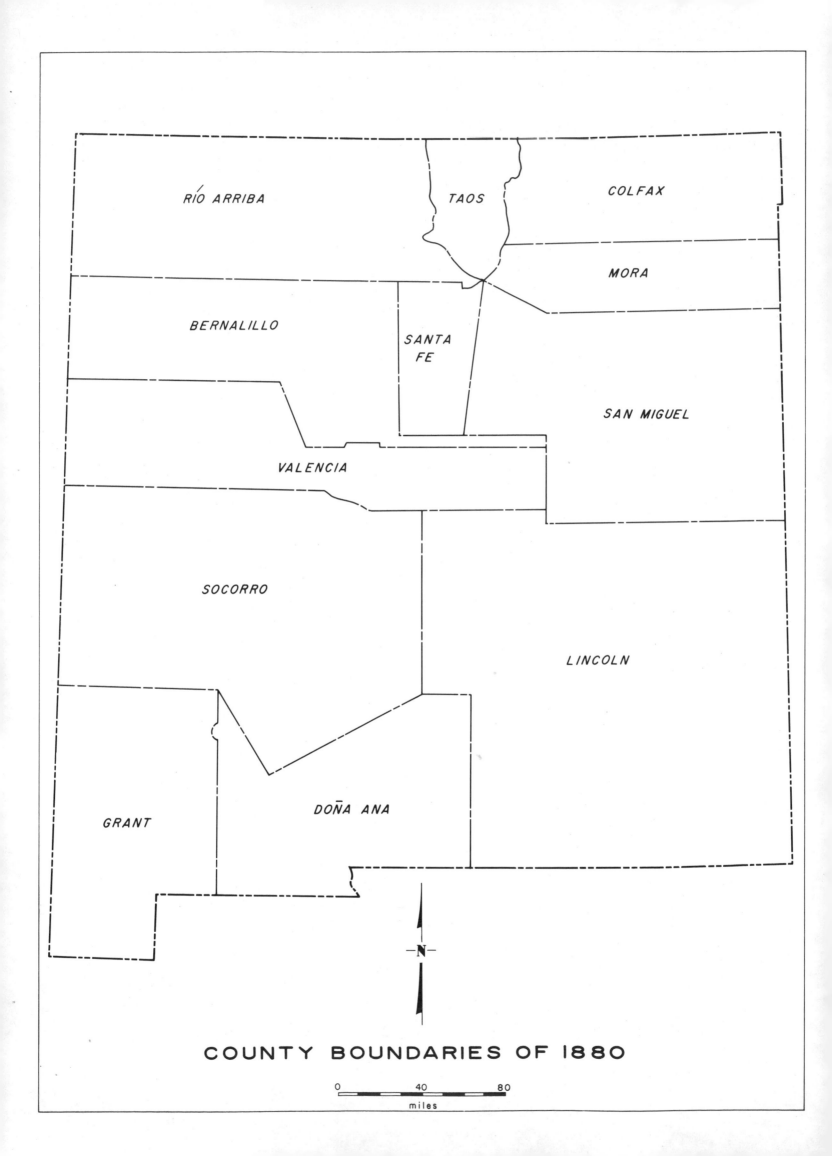

RÍO ARRIBA

TAOS

COLFAX

MORA

BERNALILLO

SANTA FE

SAN MIGUEL

VALENCIA

SOCORRO

LINCOLN

GRANT

DOÑA ANA

N

COUNTY BOUNDARIES OF 1880

0   40   80
miles

IN 1871 the Socorro–Doña Ana County boundary was altered, the new line running southeastwardly from the northeastern corner of Grant County to one mile south of Caballo Mountain in the Jornada del Muerto, and then to the eastern boundary of Doña Ana–Socorro County. In 1876, Santa Ana County was annexed to Bernalillo County and thus became the only original county to disappear from the map. The boundary between Mora County and Colfax County was redefined in 1876, the new line running from the eastern border of New Mexico through the center of Township Twenty-three north to the Taos County line.

Lincoln County was enlarged in 1878 to include within its boundaries the eastern part of Doña Ana County. The boundary followed the southern line of Lincoln County to the parallel of 28° 30′, and followed that line to the Texas border on the south. All territory east of this line became a part of Lincoln County. The western part of Taos County was annexed to Río Arriba County in 1880. This included all of the area west of the western side of the public road running from Hot Springs to the Río Arriba County line, and thence toward Conejos in Colorado as far as the New Mexico border. Further adjustments were made in the county line in 1880. The boundary between Socorro County and Doña Ana County was changed in 1880. In the

same year, the eastern line of Grant County was altered also.

In 1882 the boundary between Mora County and San Miguel County was revised. Adjustments were also made in the eastern boundary of Santa Fe County. Sierra County was carved out of parts of Socorro, Grant, and Doña Ana counties in 1884. The previously existing San Juan County was re-created out of the western part of Río Arriba County in 1887. In the same year, changes were also made in the boundaries of Doña Ana County.

In 1889 extensive county boundary changes were made. The Mora and San Miguel County boundary line was altered, as was that between Doña Ana and Lincoln counties. Chaves County and Eddy County were created in 1889 from the eastern part of Lincoln County. All of Lincoln County east of the following line was cut off. The line started at the northern border of Lincoln County between Ranges Nineteen and Twenty east, running south of the First Standard Parallel, thence directly south between Ranges Twenty and Twenty-one, east through the Third Standard Parallel, thence east to a point where the range line south of the Third Standard Parallel between Ranges Twenty-one and Twenty-two strikes the same, thence due south to the Texas border.

45. COUNTY BOUNDARIES OF 1880

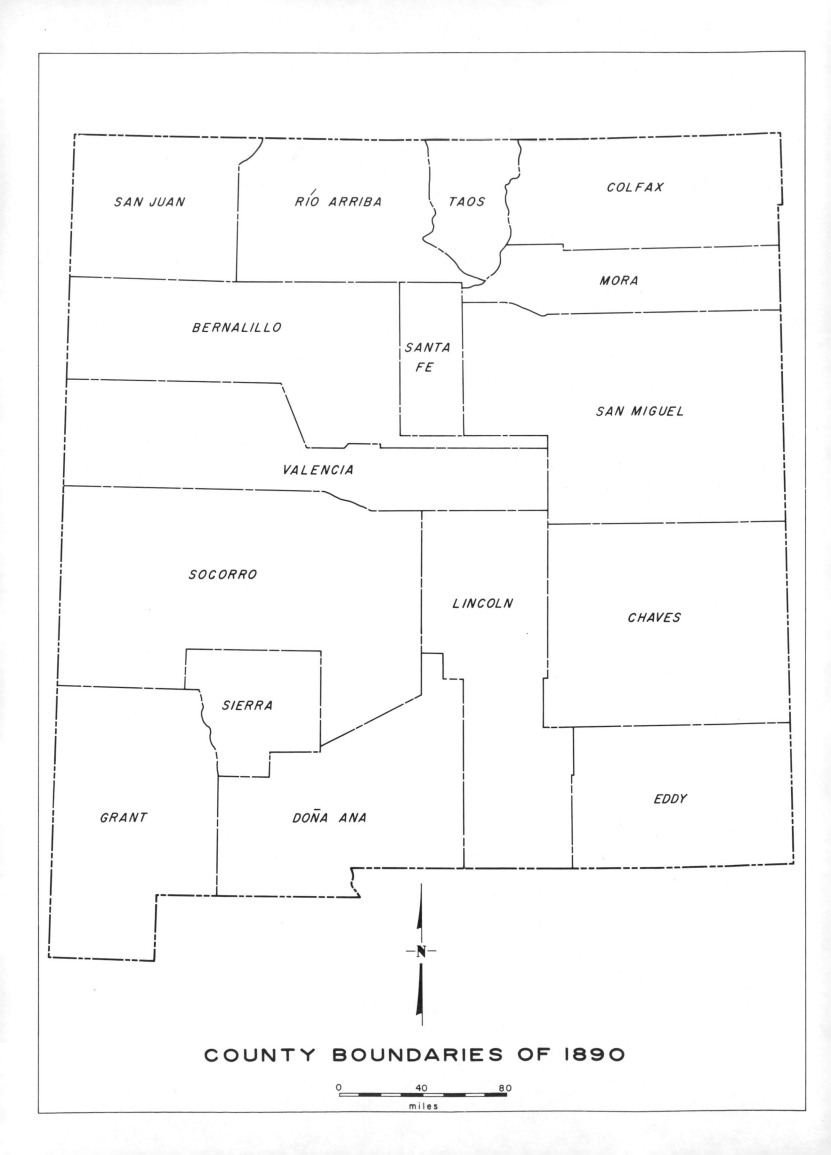

SAN JUAN

RÍO ARRIBA

TAOS

COLFAX

MORA

BERNALILLO

SANTA
FE

SAN MIGUEL

VALENCIA

SOCORRO

LINCOLN

CHAVES

SIERRA

EDDY

GRANT

DOÑA ANA

N

COUNTY BOUNDARIES OF 1890

0   40   80
miles

46. COUNTY BOUNDARIES OF 1890

(A description of this map is included in the discussion on the preceding page.)

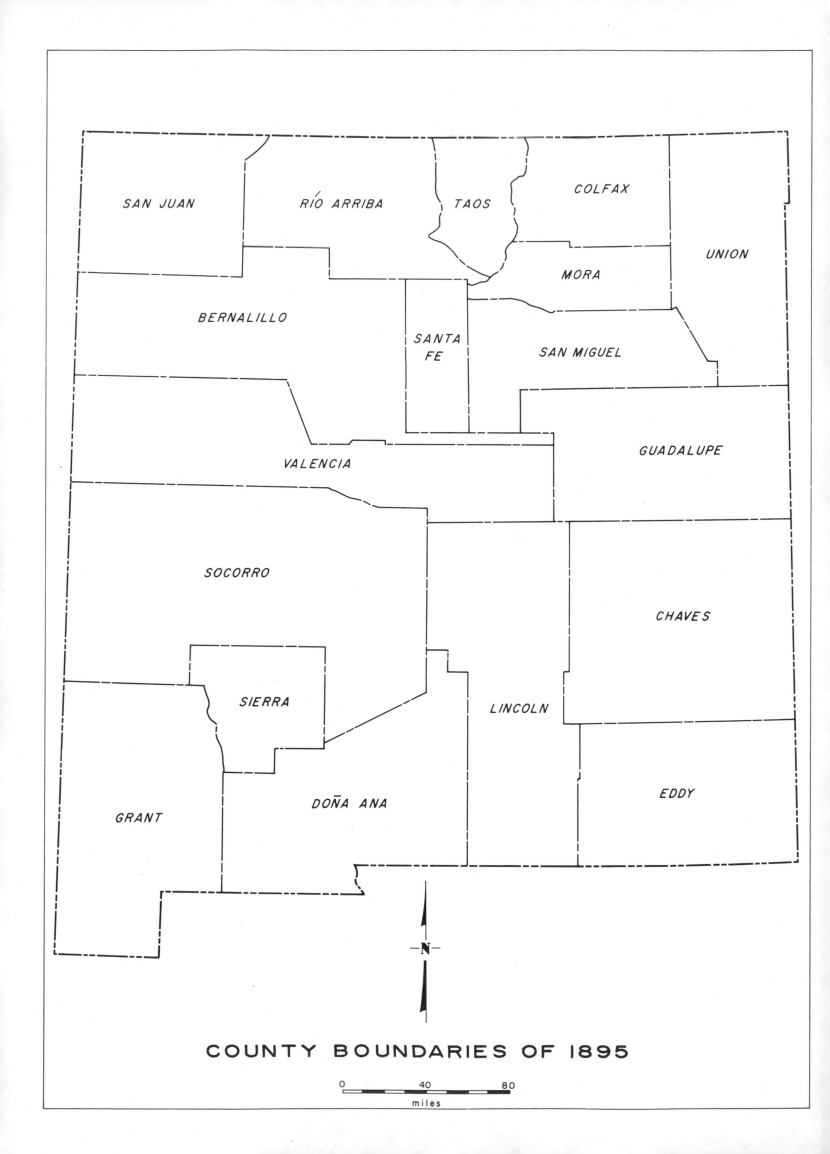

COUNTY BOUNDARIES OF 1895

0   40   80
miles

47–48. COUNTY BOUNDARIES OF 1895 AND 1900

THE SOUTHERN PART of San Miguel County was used to create Guadalupe County in 1891. It was bounded on the east by the Texas state line, on the south by Chaves and a very small corner of Lincoln County, on the west by Valencia and Bernalillo counties, and, naturally, on the north by San Miguel County. In 1893 the northern and eastern boundaries of Lincoln County were again altered. In the same year Union County was created from the eastern parts of San Miguel, Mora, and Colfax counties. In 1895 the western boundary of Eddy County and the eastern and northern boundaries of Bernalillo County were altered. In 1897 the only recently created Guadalupe County had its western boundary altered.

The year 1899 saw extensive changes in county boundary lines. Otero County was created out of the southern part of Lincoln County, the eastern part of Doña Ana County, and the southeastern corner of Socorro County. Chaves County was further enlarged in 1899 with the addition of that part of Lincoln County south of the line between Townships Thirteen and Fourteen not included in Otero County.

McKinley County was organized in 1899 also. It was bounded on the north by San Juan County, on the east by the line which ran south from the San Juan County line between Ranges Eight and Nine west, thence west along this line to the Arizona line.

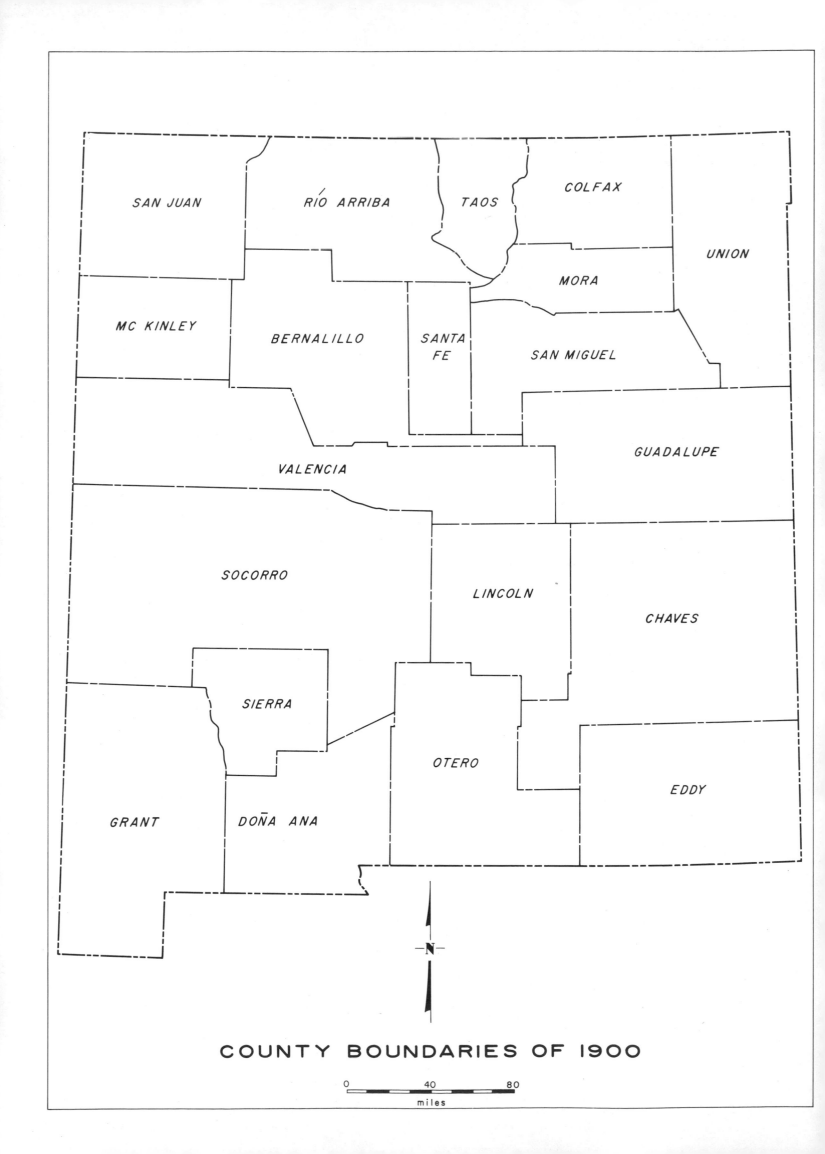

COUNTY BOUNDARIES OF 1900

0   40   80
miles

48. COUNTY BOUNDARIES OF 1900

(A description of this map is included in the discussion on the preceding page.)

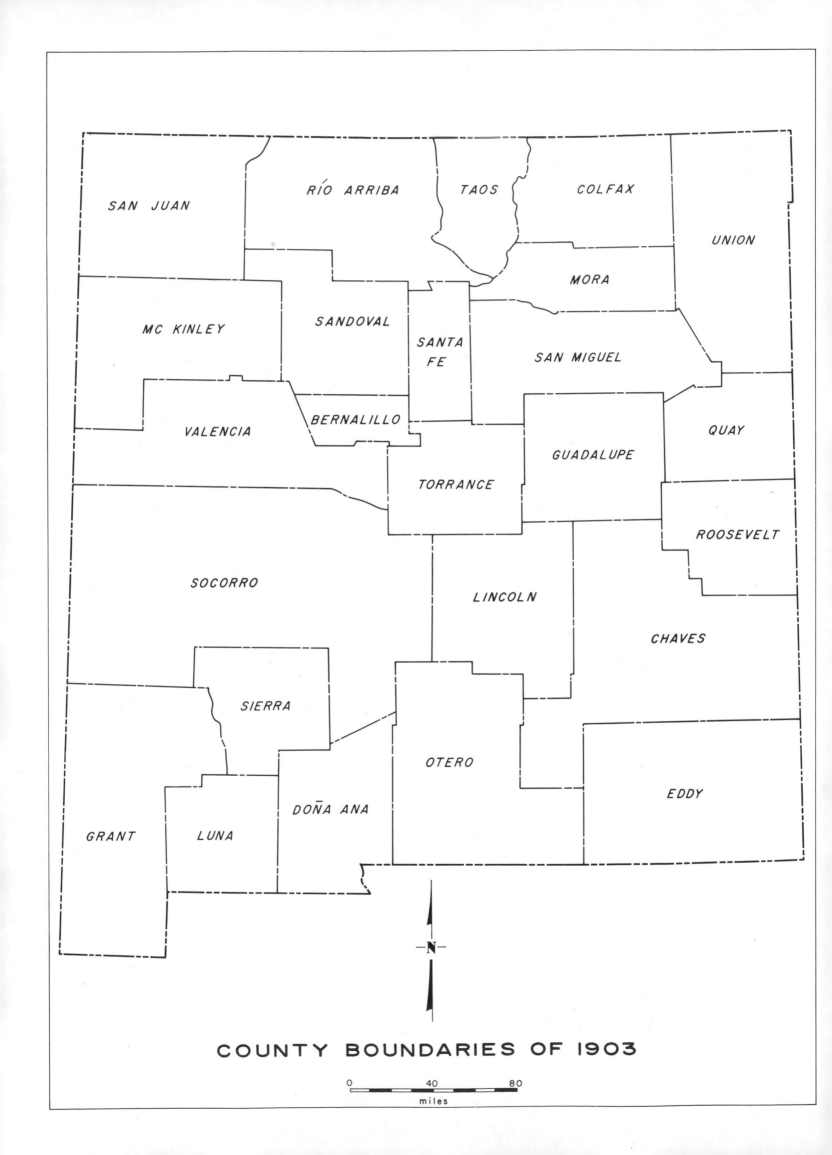

COUNTY BOUNDARIES OF 1903

SAN JUAN

RÍO ARRIBA

TAOS

COLFAX

UNION

MORA

MC KINLEY

SANDOVAL

SANTA FE

SAN MIGUEL

VALENCIA

BERNALILLO

QUAY

GUADALUPE

TORRANCE

SOCORRO

LINCOLN

ROOSEVELT

CHAVES

SIERRA

OTERO

EDDY

GRANT

LUNA

DOÑA ANA

-N-

0   40   80
miles

LUNA COUNTY WAS ORGANIZED in 1901 from the eastern part of Grant County and the western part of Doña Ana County. The same year, McKinley County was enlarged by the addition of part of western Bernalillo County and part of northern Valencia County.

Quay County was created in 1903 from the southern part of Union County and the eastern part of Guadalupe County. Roosevelt County was organized in 1903, the original county including the southeastern part of Guadalupe County and the northeastern part of Chaves County. Sandoval County was created the same year out of the north-ern part of Bernalillo County. Torrance County was created in 1903 also. It included the eastern part of Valencia County, the eastern part of Bernalillo County, the northeastern corner of Socorro County, and the northwestern part of Lincoln County.

Leonard Wood was the name applied to Guadalupe County in 1903. In 1905, however, the name was changed back to Guadalupe County. In 1905 the boundary between Taos County and Río Arriba County was slightly altered. In 1909, Curry County was made from the southeastern part of Quay County and the northeastern portion of Roosevelt County.

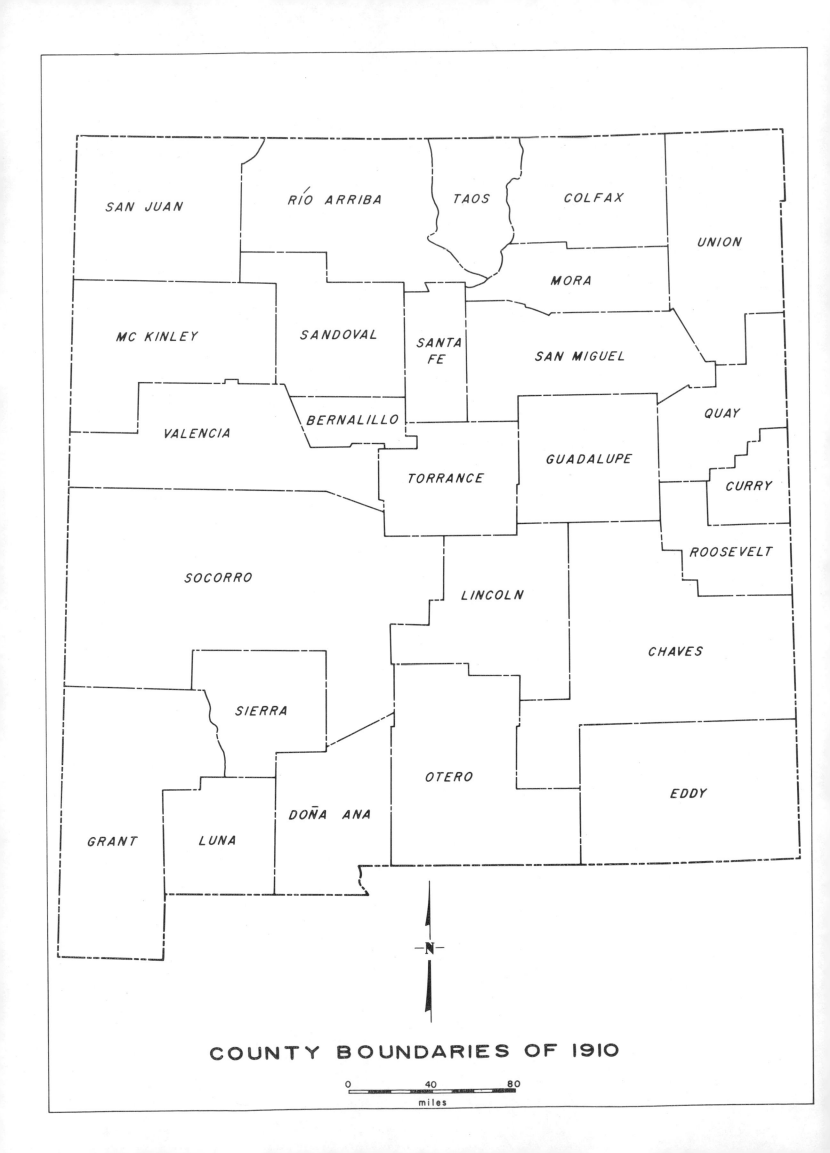

COUNTY BOUNDARIES OF 1910

0   40   80
miles

50. COUNTY BOUNDARIES OF 1910

(A description of this map is included in the discussion on the preceding page.)

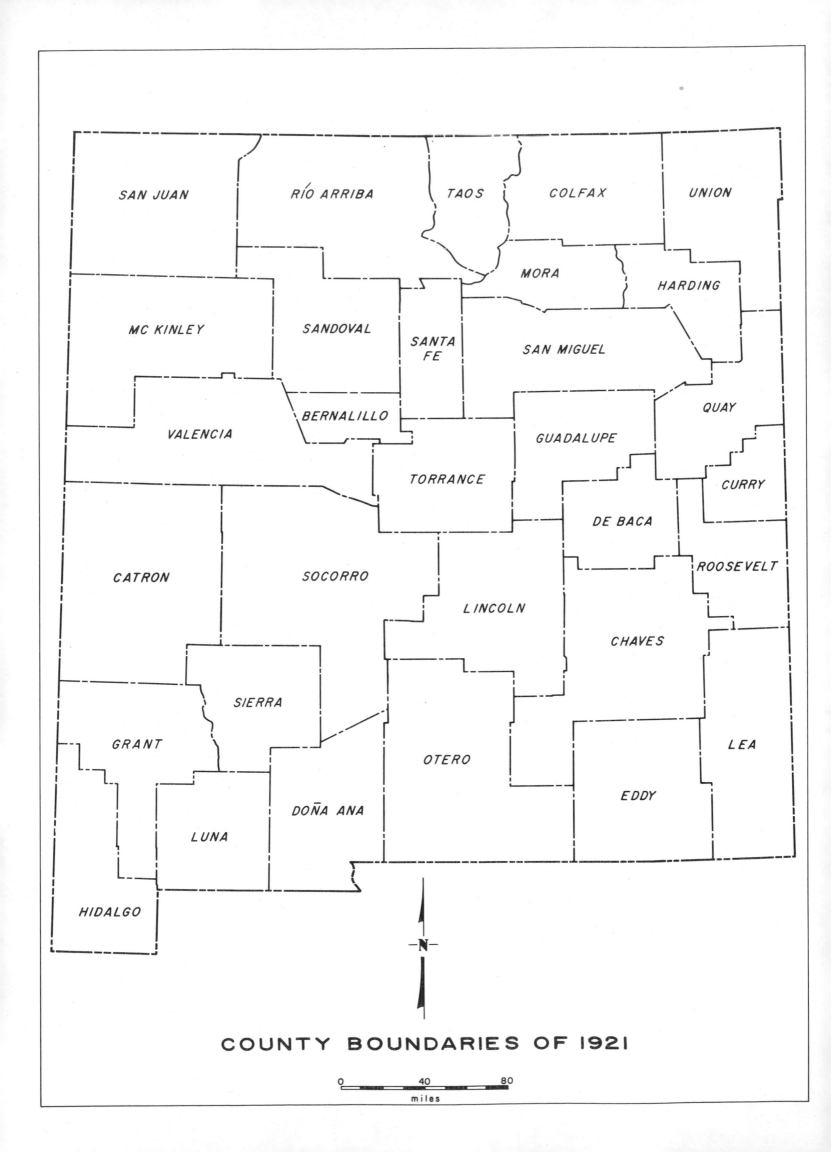

COUNTY BOUNDARIES OF 1921

N

0   40   80
miles

51-52. COUNTY BOUNDARIES OF 1921 AND THE PRESENT

DE BACA COUNTY WAS ORGANIZED in 1917 from parts of Chaves County, Guadalupe County, and Roosevelt County. In the same year the boundaries of Roosevelt County were again altered. The eastern part of the county was made a part of De Baca County, and the northeastern part of Chaves County was made a part of Roosevelt County. In 1917 also, Lea County was created from the eastern parts of Chaves and Eddy counties. Hidalgo County was created out of the southern part of Grant County in 1919.

Most of the changes in county boundaries in New Mexico were apparently completed in 1921, with only a few more to be made later. In that year Catron was organized from the western part of Socorro County, and Harding was created from a part of eastern Mora County and a part of southern Union County. The continual shifting of county lines was no longer possible after statehood, because one section of the state constitution prohibited the legislature from enacting laws affecting county boundaries except when creating new counties. The action of the state legislature creating De Baca and Lea counties in 1917, Hidalgo County in 1919, and Catron and Harding counties in 1921, did not in-volve a change of county lines in violation of the constitutional provision. In 1923, however, and again in 1927, attempts to alter county make-up were never completed. In 1947 the legislature passed a law authorizing one county to annex portions of another county. It was necessary to have a petition signed by 51 per cent of the electors residing within the affected area before the board of county commissioners could call an election there. Following a favorable vote, such an area would become a part of the adjoining county the following year. As an outgrowth of this law, slight boundary changes have been made between Socorro and Sierra counties, Harding and Quay counties, and San Miguel and Harding counties.

The last significant change in the county boundary structure of New Mexico took place as a result of World War II. During the war the federal government acquired exclusive jurisdiction of portions of Santa Fe and Sandoval counties for use by Los Alamos atomic energy project. In 1949 the federal government turned the administration of this area over to the state of New Mexico, and as a result the new county of Los Alamos was created.

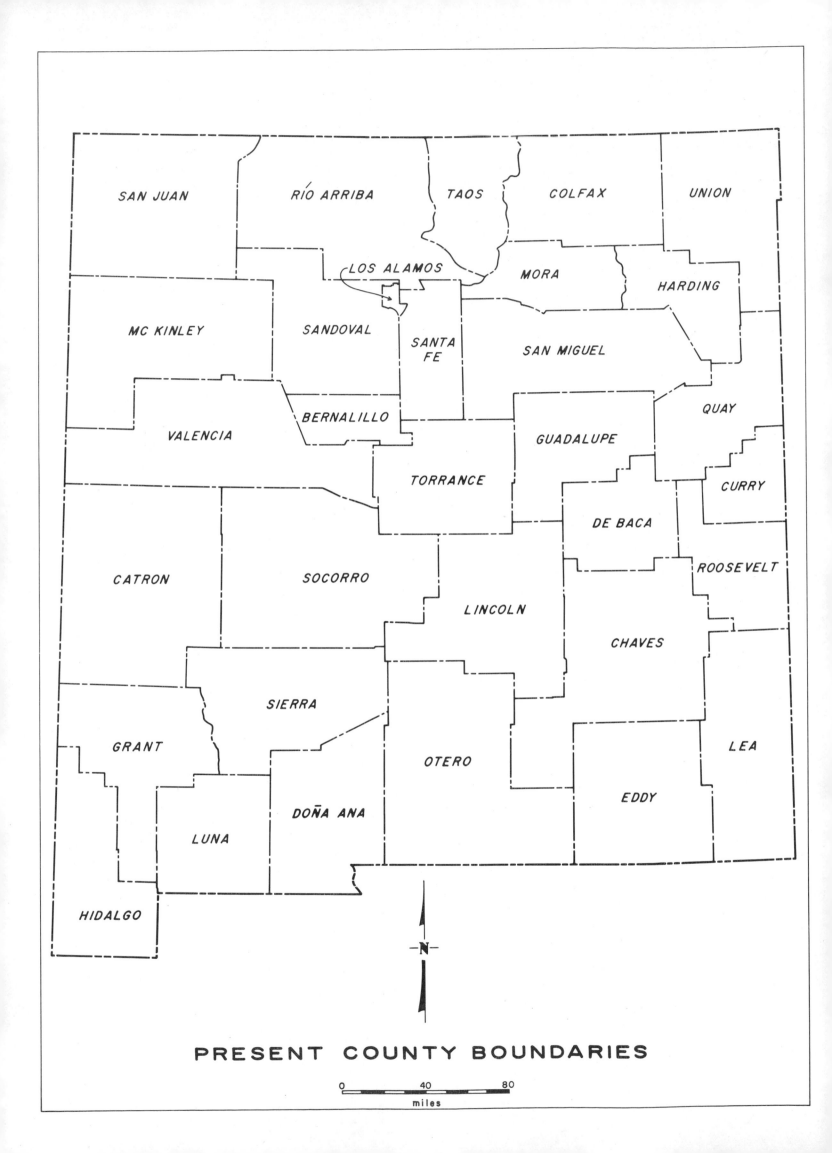

PRESENT COUNTY BOUNDARIES

0   40   80
miles

52. PRESENT COUNTY BOUNDARIES

(A description of this map is included in the discussion on the preceding page.)

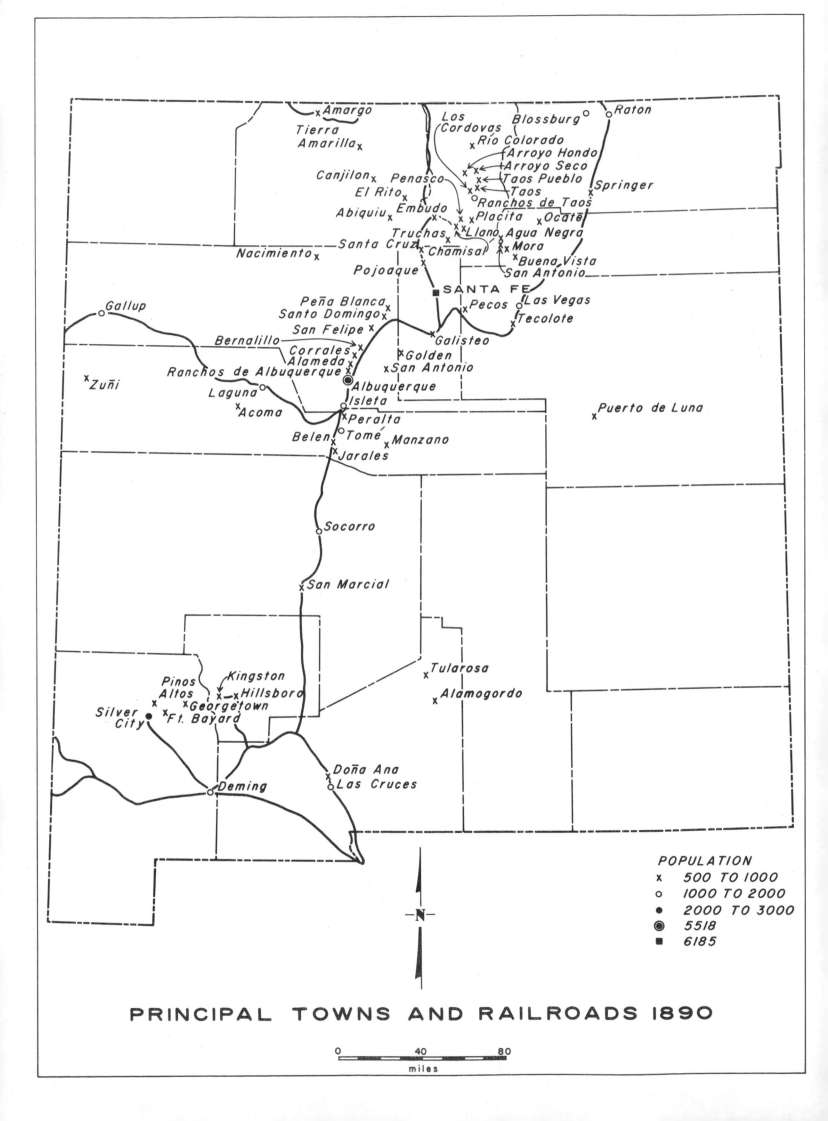

Amargo ×
Tierra
Amarilla ×
Los
Cordovas
Blossburg ○
Raton ○
Río Colorado ×
Arroyo Hondo ×
Arroyo Seco ×
Canjilon ×
Penasco
Taos Pueblo ×
Springer ×
El Rito ×
Taos ×
Abiquiu ×
Embudo
Placita ×
Ranchos de Taos ×
Ocaté ×
Truchas ×
Llano
Agua Negra
Santa Cruz ×
Chamisal ×
Mora ×
Nacimiento ×
Buena Vista ×
Pojoaque
San Antonio
SANTA FE ■
Peña Blanca ×
Pecos ×
Las Vegas ○
Gallup ○
Santo Domingo ×
Tecolote ×
Bernalillo
San Felipe ×
Corrales ×
Galisteo ×
Alameda ×
Golden ×
Ranchos de Albuquerque ×
San Antonio ×
Zuñi ×
Albuquerque ◎
Puerto de Luna ×
Laguna ○
Isleta ○
Acoma ×
Peralta ×
Belen ×
Tomé ○
Manzano ×
Jarales ×

Socorro ○

San Marcial ×

Kingston ×
Tularosa ×
Pinos
Altos ×
Hillsboro ×
Georgetown ×
Alamogordo ×
Silver
City ●
Ft. Bayard ×

Doña Ana ×
Deming ○
Las Cruces ○

POPULATION
× 500 TO 1000
○ 1000 TO 2000
● 2000 TO 3000
◎ 5518
■ 6185

N

PRINCIPAL TOWNS AND RAILROADS 1890

0   40   80
miles

53. PRINCIPAL TOWNS AND RAILROADS, 1890

By 1890 the traditional pattern of New Mexico's populace clinging to the banks of the Río Grande and its tributaries began to shift. Although most people still were to be found in the areas populated by their fathers, new forces were prompting a change.

The coming of the railroad made it feasible to transport men and goods into areas once relatively inaccessible. The railroads themselves created new towns, such as Raton, Gallup, Deming, and others.

Mining was also a compelling force, causing people to move to previously uninhabited parts of New Mexico. Gold mining in Colfax, Taos, Mora, and other counties was the magnet that drew people into these areas. Silver mining in Sierra and Grant counties and coal mining near Raton and Gallup were equally magnetic. But in spite of these changes, the state's population remained overwhelmingly rural, 93.8 per cent of the people falling into this classification. The eastern third of the state remained virtually unpopulated. The area could not be effectively settled until the railroad came.

The coming of the railroad to New Mexico in 1879 reduced reliance upon cart roads and trails which had served the state since the Spanish came in 1598. Stagecoaches and freight wagons remained as feeder transportation, serving areas not yet reached by the railroad. Some of these lasted until the motor vehicle replaced them.

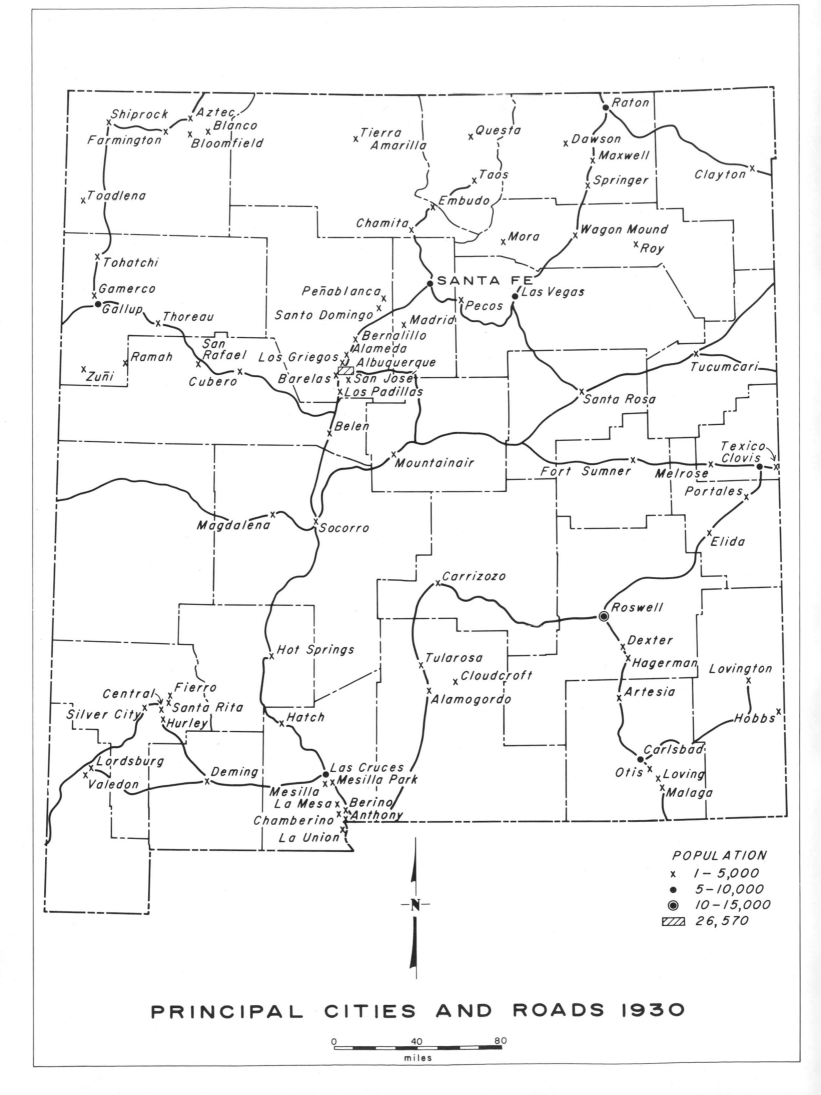

Shiprock Aztec
Farmington Blanco
  Bloomfield

Toadlena

Tierra Questa
Amarilla

Taos

Embudo

Chamita

Raton
Dawson
  Maxwell
Springer

Clayton

Tohatchi

Gamerco
Gallup Thoreau

Ramah
San
Rafael Los Griegos
Zuñi

Cubero Barelas

Peñablanca
Santo Domingo
  Madrid
Bernalillo
Alameda
Albuquerque
San Jose
Los Padillas

Belen

Mora
Wagon Mound
  Roy

SANTA FE
Pecos
Las Vegas

Tucumcari

Santa Rosa

Magdalena Socorro

Mountainair

Fort Sumner Melrose

Texico
Clovis

Portales

Elida

Carrizozo

Hot Springs

Fierro
Central Santa Rita
Silver City Hurley

Hatch

Tularosa
Cloudcroft
Alamogordo

Roswell

Dexter
Hagerman

Artesia

Lovington

Hobbs

Lordsburg
Valedon Deming

Mesilla
La Mesa Las Cruces
Mesilla Park

Berino
Chamberino Anthony
La Union

Carlsbad

Otis Loving
  Malaga

POPULATION
x   1 – 5,000
•   5 – 10,000
⊙   10 – 15,000
▨   26,570

N

PRINCIPAL CITIES AND ROADS 1930

0   40   80
miles

THE POPULATION OF NEW MEXICO reached 423,317 in 1930, representing an 18 per cent increase over 1920. Nineteen counties showed gains, and ten lost population. Those counties declined which still had ranching or farming economic bases. Those gaining did so because of oil or irrigated farming. Most of the gains, however, were in the cities, at the expense of the countryside. Urban area population increased 64 per cent. Rural population increased only 7 per cent. Nevertheless, New Mexico remained a rural state, 74.8 per cent of her population falling into this category. Albuquerque, the only large city in the state, received much of the increase.

The advent of the motor car in the 1930's reduced dependence on the railroad. Highways were rapidly built, connecting the leading cities or fitting into the transcontinental road pattern. Because the state had much mountainous terrain, the cost of building was very high, and, consequently, the secondary road pattern was inadequate in 1930. Even with this hindrance, however, the motor vehicle was indispensable in a state whose size had historically hampered transportation.

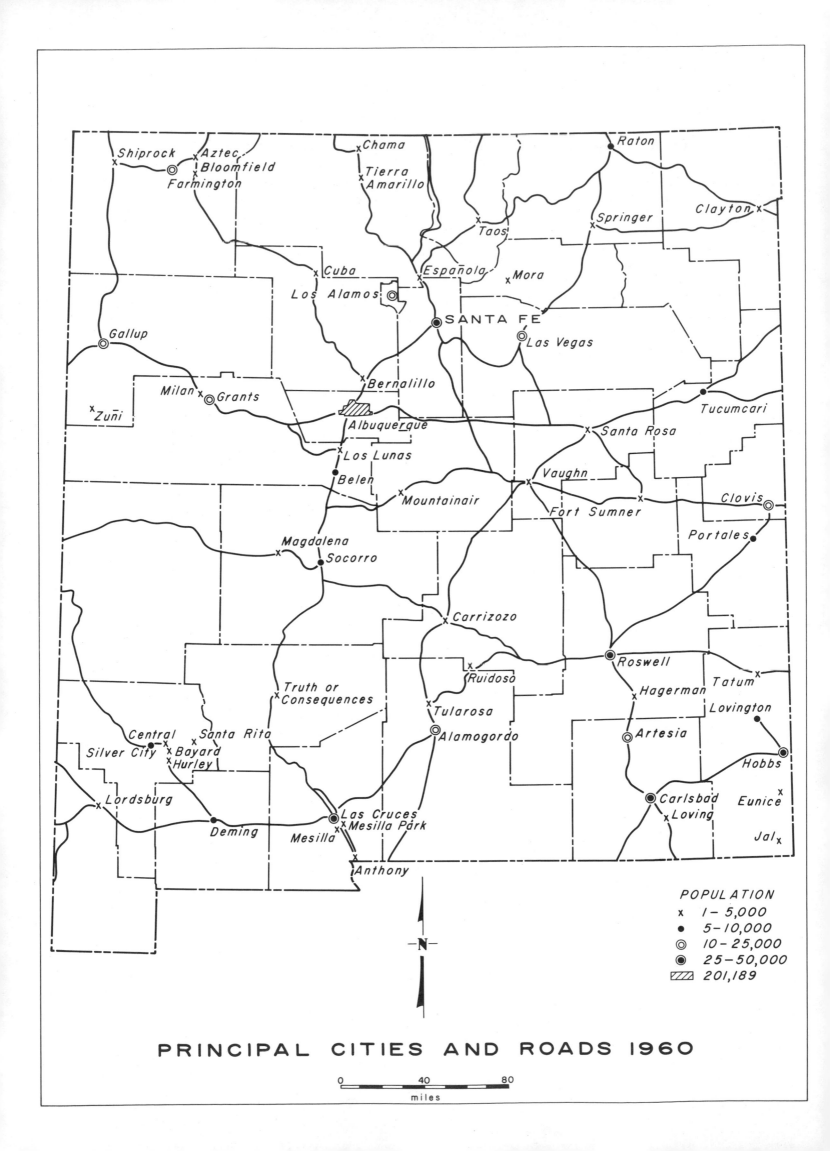

Shiprock
x

Aztec
x
Bloomfield
◎
Farmington

Chama
x

Tierra
Amarillo

Raton
●

Clayton
x

Taos
x

Springer
x

Gallup
◎

Cuba
x

Española
◎

Mora
x

Los Alamos
◎

SANTA FE
●

Las Vegas
◎

Milan
x
Grants
◎

Zuñi
x

Bernalillo
x

Albuquerque
▨

Tucumcari
●

Los Lunas
x

Santa Rosa
x

Belen
●

Vaughn
x

Clovis
◎

Mountainair
x

Fort Sumner
x

Portales
●

Magdalena
x
Socorro
●

Carrizozo
x

Roswell
◉

Tatum
x

Ruidoso
x

Hagerman
x

Truth or
Consequences
x

Lovington
●

Tularosa
x

Alamogordo
◎

Artesia
◎

Central
x
Santa Rita
x

Silver City
x
Bayard
x
Hurley
x

Hobbs
◉

Lordsburg
x

Las Cruces
◉
Mesilla Park
x

Carlsbad
●
Eunice
x

Deming
●

Mesilla
x

Loving
x

Jal
x

Anthony
x

POPULATION

x 1 – 5,000
● 5 – 10,000
◎ 10 – 25,000
◉ 25 – 50,000
▨ 201,189

N

PRINCIPAL CITIES AND ROADS 1960

0   40   80
miles

55. PRINCIPAL CITIES AND ROADS, 1960

IN 1960, New Mexico had a population of 951,023. Of this total, 510,454 resided in seventeen metropolitan centers of more than 8,000 each. Twenty-seven per cent of this total lived in a single county, Bernalillo (Albuquerque). The 39.6 per cent population growth in the previous decade occurred exclusively in the cities, rural areas losing population. While most of the state shared in this growth, the most pronounced increase was in the southeastern and northwestern portions. By 1960 only 34.1 per cent of the state's inhabitants were rural dwellers. The state's population conformed to the national trend toward urbanization.

Rapid increase in the state's population and its concentration in urban centers resulted from a variety of factors. The many federal projects which came to New Mexico after World War II helped attract private industry. In addition, uranium mining, increase in oil and gas production, and expansion of atomic research and special weapons pro-grams, plus retention of wartime military installations, created greater economic opportunity, and thus attracted many people.

By 1960 the former isolation of New Mexico from the rest of the nation, as well as within the state, had all but disappeared. The state remained a well-traversed area with modern high-speed highways bringing travelers from all over the nation into New Mexico. Since 1930 many additional miles of highway had been built or improved. Some of these roads were in the southeast or the northwest, reflecting the increased population in these areas. Others, such as the road from Alamogordo to Las Cruces, connected important cities through mountain terrain. Still other routes were built to shorten transcontinental roads. More important, an extensive network of all-weather roads made travel to the many attractive tourist sites easily possible. Only a few areas are not now accessible.

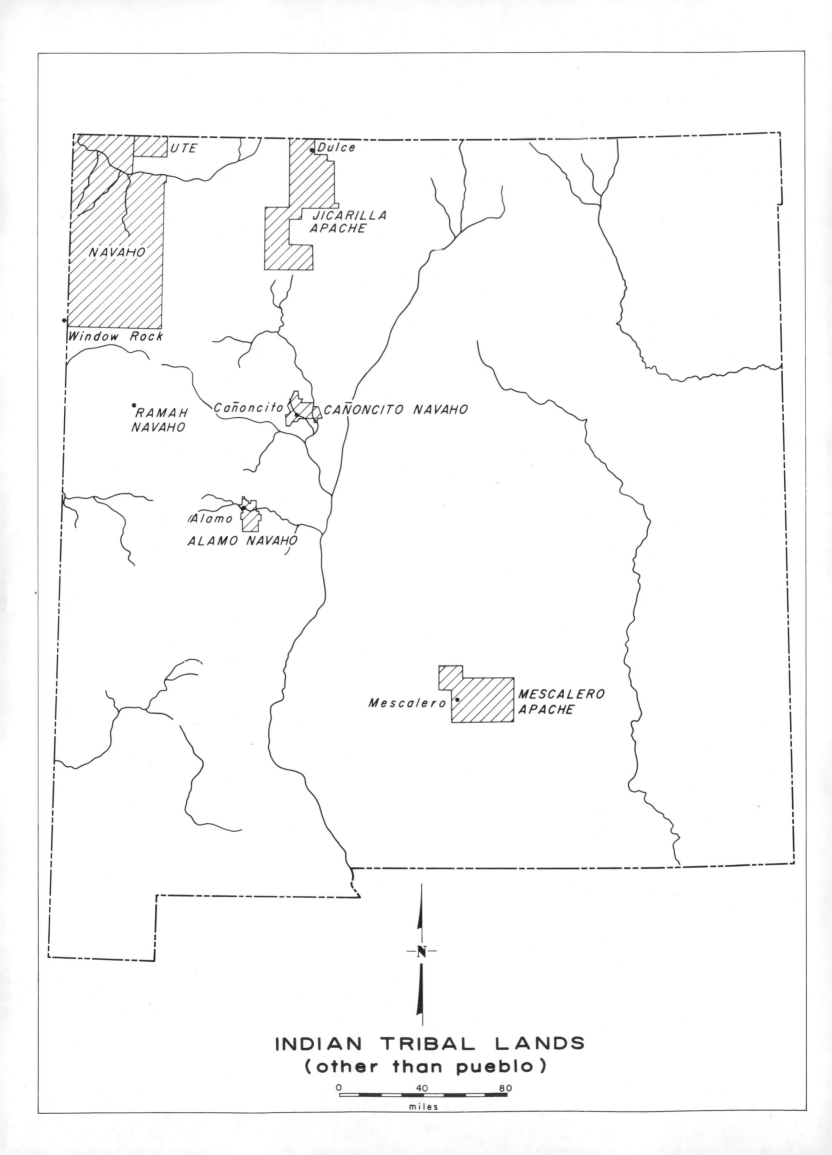

UTE

•Dulce

NAVAHO

JICARILLA
APACHE

•Window Rock

•RAMAH
NAVAHO

Cañoncito   CAÑONCITO NAVAHO

Alamo
ALAMO NAVAHO

Mescalero•   MESCALERO
APACHE

—N—

INDIAN TRIBAL LANDS
(other than pueblo)

0   40   80
miles

THE LARGEST INDIAN GROUP in New Mexico besides the Pueblos are the Navahos—39,000 of whom live there. Most of them live on 3,500,000 acres of reservation land in the northwestern part of the state, but there are three other widely scattered groups. They are the Ramahs at Ramah, who number 1,000; the Cañoncitos west of Albuquerque, about 836; and the Alamos north of Magdalena, about 799. The Navahos are governed by a 74-member tribal council. Their capital is Window Rock, Arizona.

Their traditional economic activity—keeping sheep and cattle—has been drastically altered in recent years. The $8,000,000 yearly income from oil, gas, and uranium lease rentals has made possible many improvements upon their lands. Additional income from the tourist trade and the exploitation of timber resources help care for the increasing population. But despite economic changes, the Navahos have managed to preserve most of their rituals and arts.

The Jicarilla Apaches (named by the Spaniards for their ability to make baskets which could be used for drinking cups) today number some 1,548 on a 722,303-acre reservation. They are divided into the Ollero Mountain people and the Llanero Plains people. They are governed by their own 8-man tribal council.

They have income from the recreation areas of Dulce and La Jara, graze sizable herds of cattle, and operate their own sawmills. Like the Navahos, the Jicarillas also derive income from gas and oil.

The Mescalero Apaches have a population of 1,300 who live on a reservation area of 460,000 acres. They too are governed by a tribal committee of 10 people. Farming, stock-raising, and timber cutting are the major economic activities. The important national highway that goes through their reservation has helped promote tourist trade. Large recreation centers like Ruidoso and the Holloman Air Development Center near Alamogordo furnish jobs. Providing Christmas trees for near-by areas is an industry, but the area's best-known "workers" are the famous Red Hats. This is a group of volunteer fire fighters who wear a distinctive red-striped helmet and have been effectively used all over the West.

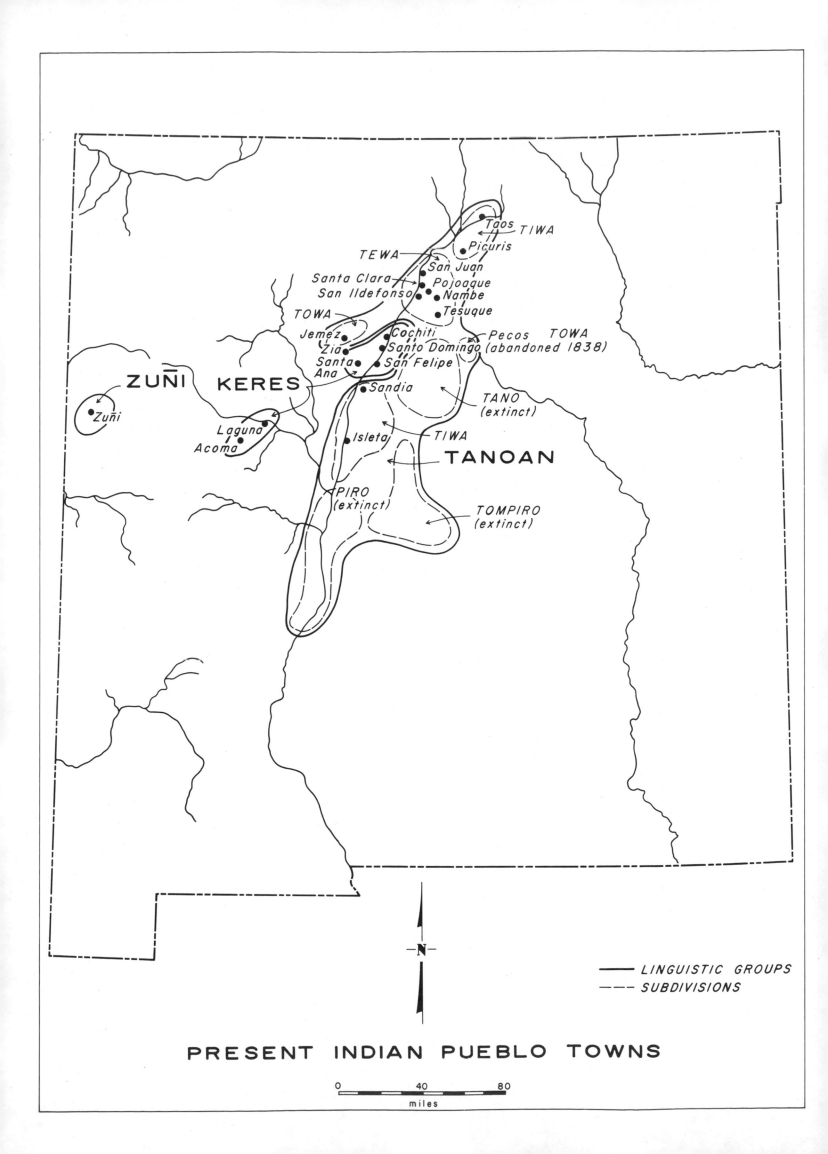

Taos — TIWA

TEWA

Picuris

San Juan

Santa Clara
San Ildefonso

Pojoaque
Nambe

Tesuque

TOWA

Jemez

Cochiti

Pecos   TOWA
(abandoned 1838)

Zia

Santo Domingo

ZUÑI   KERES

Santa
Ana

San Felipe

Sandia

TANO
(extinct)

Zuñi

Laguna

Acoma

Isleta

TIWA

TANOAN

PIRO
(extinct)

TOMPIRO
(extinct)

N

LINGUISTIC GROUPS

SUBDIVISIONS

PRESENT INDIAN PUEBLO TOWNS

0   40   80
miles

57. PRESENT INDIAN PUEBLO TOWNS

In 1964, 19,556 Pueblo Indians lived on nineteen land grants in New Mexico. For the past few years their numbers have been steadily growing, which suggests an improved ability to adjust to the changing times. They are mainly concentrated in the Río Grande Valley. The Piro sites south of Isleta, the Tano sites, and the Pecos have been abandoned as a result of assimilation and consolidation.

The Pueblos are not a single entity or tribe. Each village continues to exist, as in Spanish days, as an integral, but still autonomous, unit. Each has its own distinct administration under a governor.

At present there are three major linguistic groups—Zuñi, Keres, and Tanoan. The last has three divisions: Tewa, Towa, and Tiwa.

1. Tanoan
   Tiwa—Taos, Picuris, Sandia, and Isleta.
   Tewa—San Juan, Santa Clara, San Ildefonso, Tesuque, Pojoaque, and Nambe.
   Towa—Jemez, and also formerly at Pecos.
2. Keres—Acoma, Laguna, Zia, Santa Ana, San Felipe, Santo Domingo, and Cochiti.
3. Zuñi

The languages are so dissimilar that neighboring pueblos have found it easier to communicate in English or Spanish.

Pueblo Indians are basically farmers, but have added sheep and cattle grazing to their activities. They also are skilled in handicrafts, such as pottery, weaving, basketry, jewelry-making, and leatherwork. Some villages have earned enviable reputations for the excellence of their products. The tourist provides a market for such goods, and helps the Indians preserve their native crafts. Vocational training helps many Indians obtain jobs at Los Alamos or Albuquerque, and others even leave the pueblos to find work in distant places.

FACTS ABOUT NEW MEXICO'S PUEBLOS

Reservation Name	Linguistic Group	Population (1964)	Reservation Area (Acres)	Period of Occupation (Years)
Acoma	Keresan	1,674	248,000	1,000
Cochiti	Keresan	387	26,500	700
Isleta	Tiwa	1,974	210,450	400
Jemez	Towa	1,076	87,000	400
Laguna	Keresan	2,956	412,000	265
Nambe	Tewa	135	19,000	650
Picuris	Tiwa	100	15,000	760
Pojoaque	Tewa	41	12,000	——
Sandia	Tiwa	124	23,000	660
San Felipe	Keresan	1,060	49,000	250
San Ildefonso	Tewa	224	26,000	660
San Juan	Tewa	690	13,000	660
Santa Ana	Keresan	366	20,000	260
Santa Clara	Tewa	535	46,000	600
Santo Domingo	Keresan	1,938	67,000	260
Taos	Tiwa	896	47,000	260
Tesuque	Tewa	142	17,000	660
Zia	Keresan	377	90,000	660
Zuñi	Zuñian	4,861	400,000	270

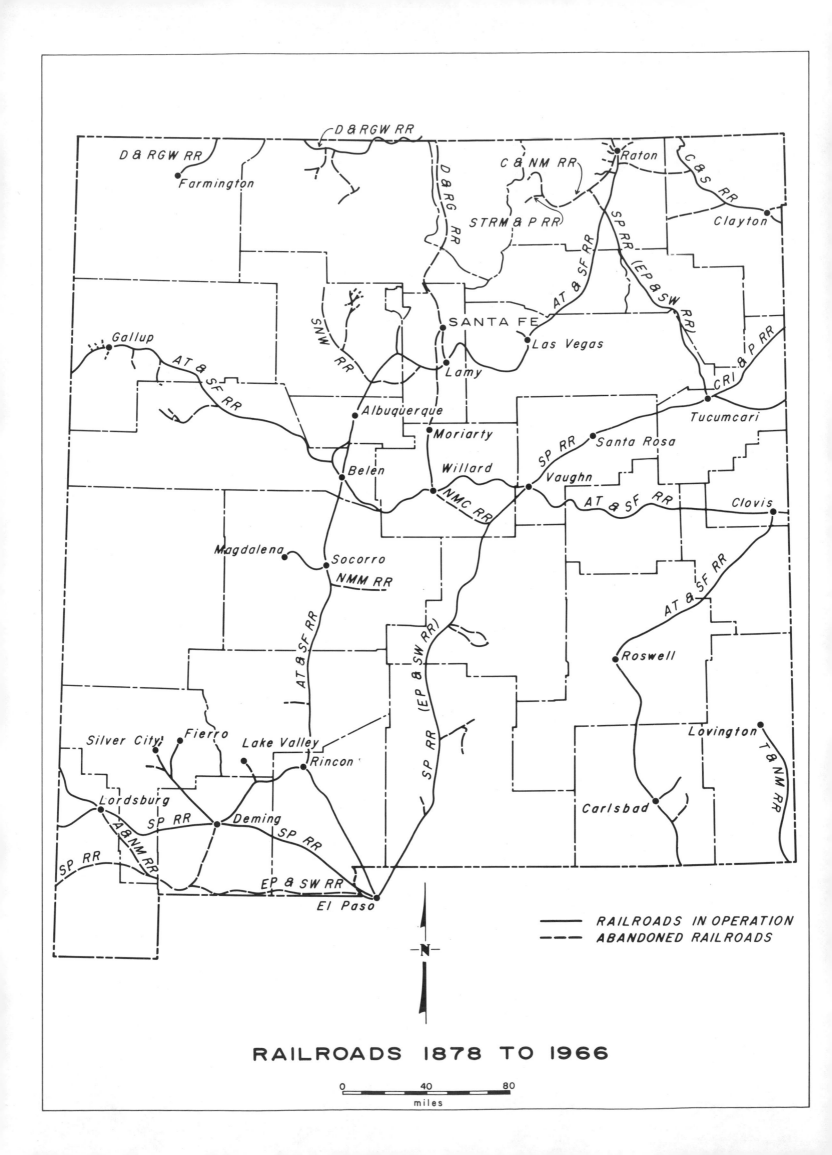

D & RGW RR
D & RGW RR
Farmington

C & NM RR
Raton
C & S RR
STRM & P RR
Clayton

D & RG RR
SP RR (EP & SW RR)
AT & SF RR
SANTA FE
Las Vegas

SNW RR
CRI & P RR

Gallup
AT & SF RR
Lamy
Tucumcari

Albuquerque
Moriarty

Belen
Willard
SP RR
Santa Rosa
Vaughn

NMC RR
AT & SF RR
Clovis

Magdalena
Socorro
NMM RR

SP RR (EP & SW RR)
Roswell

AT & SF RR

Silver City
Fierro
Lake Valley
Lovington
T & NM RR
Rincon

Lordsburg
SP RR
Deming
SP RR
Carlsbad
A & NM RR
SP RR
EP & SW RR
El Paso

N

——— RAILROADS IN OPERATION
– – – ABANDONED RAILROADS

RAILROADS 1878 TO 1966

0   40   80
miles

58. RAILROADS, 1878-1966

THE Atchison, Topeka, and Santa Fe Railroad was the first to reach New Mexico, and remains the most important of all carriers. Its many branches traversed the territory from the Colorado line on the north to the Texas line on the south, and from the Texas line on the east to the Arizona line on the west. Its first route followed, approximately, the old Santa Fe Trail through Raton Pass. The Santa Fe had planned to use the southern route westward to California, and constructed its road south from Albuquerque to Deming. However, the Southern Pacific had reached El Paso in 1881 and did not take kindly to the efforts of the Santa Fe to parallel its route. To forestall ruinous competition, a temporary compromise was arranged between the two railroads which permitted the Santa Fe to use the Southern Pacific roadbed.

In an effort to open up the southeastern portion of the territory to settlers who would take advantage of the newly irrigated land, a group of local promoters built their own railroad. This line, the Pecos Valley Railroad, originally connected Eddy (Carlsbad) with Pecos, Texas, where it joined the Texas and Pacific line. Later it was extended northward to Roswell and then to Amarillo, Texas. In 1901 the Santa Fe acquired control of this short line.

The next step to connect this road with its other lines was for the Santa Fe to build the so-called Belen cut-off. The extension eliminated the long and hazardous journey through Raton Pass for the transcontinental trains, and constituted an obvious link in the system. The eastern junction was at the new town of Clovis, which later became an important railway center. The line was opened to through trains in 1908 and was soon hauling most of the Santa Fe transcontinental traffic.

Countless other feeder lines were built either to mines or to timber markets, but none of them played a vital role in the state's transportation system, and most of them were soon abandoned, some even being purchased by the Santa Fe. The Southern Pacific line from El Paso northward to Carrizozo, Vaughn, and Tucumcari has remained. The latter point is linked with the Rock Island Road, which built into New Mexico in 1898. Another competitor for New Mexico railroad traffic was the Denver and Río Grande. Although it did build into New Mexico, failure to obtain a right of way through Raton Pass was so costly that this line never figured prominently in the history of New Mexico railroading.

By 1914, even before railroad construction was complete in New Mexico, unprofitable lines had begun to be abandoned. This phenomenon, resulting in part from competition of highways and pipelines, was paralleled in the nation at large. In New Mexico total railway mileage has varied as follows:

Year	Mileage	Year	Mileage
1800	643	1930	2,981
1890	1,284	1945	2,538
1912	3,002	1950	2,464
1914	3,124	1963	2,164
1926	3,096		

Map Key

AT & SF—Atchison, Topeka & Santa Fe
A & NM—Arizona & New Mexico
C & NM—Colorado & New Mexico
C & S—Colorado & Southern
CRI & P—Chicago, Rock Island & Pacific
D & RG—Denver & Río Grande
D & RGW—Denver & Río Grande Western
EP & SW—El Paso & Southwestern
NMM—New Mexico Midland
NMC—New Mexico Central
SNW—Santa Fe Northwestern
SP—Southern Pacific
STRM & P—St. Louis, Rocky Mountain & Pacific
T & NM—Texas & New Mexico

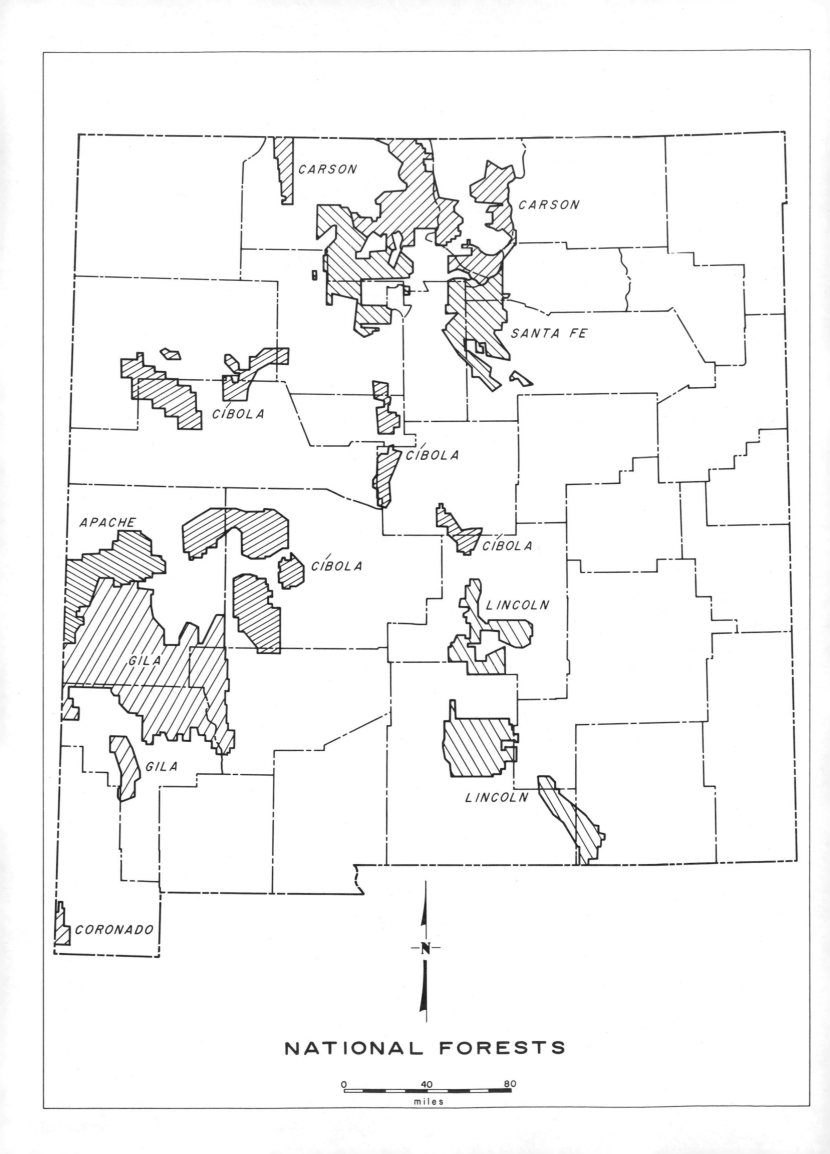

CARSON

CARSON

SANTA FE

CIBOLA

CIBOLA

APACHE

CIBOLA

CIBOLA

GILA

LINCOLN

GILA

LINCOLN

CORONADO

N

NATIONAL FORESTS

0   40   80
miles

A LARGE PERCENTAGE of the area of New Mexico has been set aside for national forests. These forests have been known by different names, and the area they cover has been altered through the years.

Coronado covers only a small area in New Mexico. Established in 1908, it was a consolidation of Dragoon, Santa Rita, and Santa Catarina. In 1917, Chiricahua was added to Coronado. Lincoln National Forest, established in 1902, has an area of 1,444,311 acres. Added to its territory were Sacramento, Alamo, Guadalupe, and Gallinas, each of which had existed briefly as an independent national forest.

Comprising 2,458,505 acres, the Gila National Forest is the largest in the state and includes areas of historic as well as scenic value. It was set up as the Gila River area in 1899. Portions of Datil and Big Burros were added to the region. Apache National Forest, adjacent to Gila, is mainly in Arizona. It was first organized in 1908, and has added to its area a part of the Datil National Forest, as well as Magdalena and San Mateo.

Cíbola was created in 1931 from the consolidation of Manzaro (1906) and Zuñi (1909). Having nine separate parts, it is widely scattered over the center of the state. Carson National Forest was established in 1908 from Taos and a portion of Jemez National Forest. Its 1,188,138 acres include some of the most rugged terrain in the state. Adjacent to Carson is Santa Fe National Forest. It includes approximately 1,200,000 acres and was established in 1915 from portions of Jemez and Pecos National Forests.

National Forest	Date Estab.	Acres	Previous Names
Gila	1899	2,458,505	Established as Gila River, Added Big Burros (1908) and part of Datil (1931)
Lincoln	1902	1,444,311	Known as Sacramento (1902), Gallinas (1905), and Guadalupe (1907) Consolidated 1908 to Alamo
Carson	1908	1,188,138	Taos (1906) and part of Jemez (1905)
Apache (N.M.–Ariz.)	1908	1,009,553 (in N.M.)	Known as Datil Forest (1908), added Magdalena (1909) and San Mateo (1908)
Coronado (N.M.–Ariz.)	1908	128,323 (in N.M.)	Peloncillo (1906) and Chiricahua (1902)
Santa Fe	1915	1,200,000	Formerly Pecos (Pecos River, 1892, first NF in N.M.) and part of Jemez (1905)
Cíbola	1931	2,275,282	Formerly Manzano (1906) and added Mt. Taylor (1908) and Zuñi (1914)

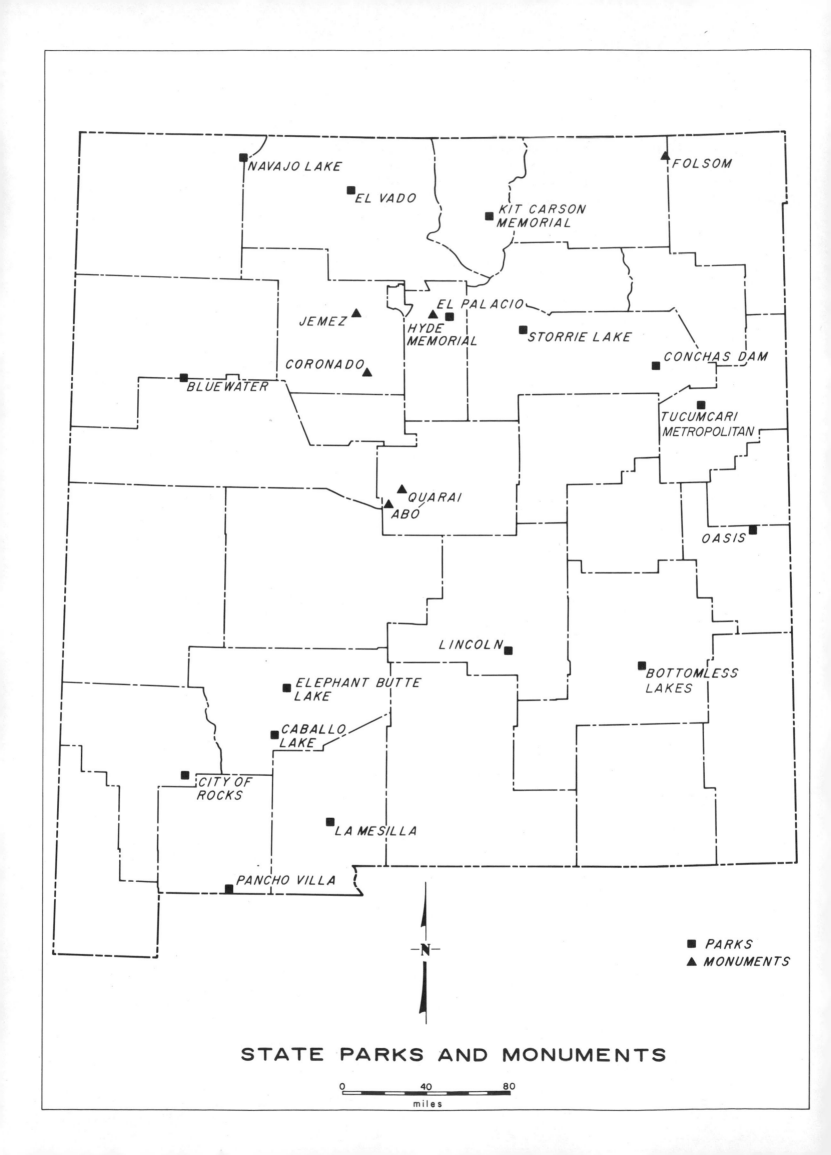

NAVAJO LAKE

FOLSOM

EL VADO

KIT CARSON
MEMORIAL

JEMEZ

EL PALACIO

HYDE
MEMORIAL

STORRIE LAKE

CORONADO

CONCHAS DAM

BLUEWATER

TUCUMCARI
METROPOLITAN

QUARAI

ABO

OASIS

LINCOLN

BOTTOMLESS
LAKES

ELEPHANT BUTTE
LAKE

CABALLO
LAKE

CITY OF
ROCKS

LA MESILLA

PANCHO VILLA

N

■ PARKS
▲ MONUMENTS

STATE PARKS AND MONUMENTS

0   40   80
miles

60. STATE PARKS AND MONUMENTS

BECAUSE OF ITS HISTORIC PAST and varied geographical conditions, New Mexico has many outstanding state monuments and state parks. At Folsom a state monument marks the site where artifacts of prehistoric man were discovered.

The Jemez State Monument contains the ruins of the mission of San José de Jemez. At one time a thriving pueblo, it was abandoned in 1622. The near-by Coronado State Monument is near the site of two pre-Columbian Tiguex pueblo ruins. Other pre-Columbian ruins are at Quarai State Monument. This was once an important walled city but was abandoned about 1674. Abó State Monument is the site of Piro Indian Pueblo ruins which had been abandoned prior to the Pueblo Revolt of 1680 because of Apache raids. El Palacio State Monument in Santa Fe, the former home of the Spanish governors, which has figured so prominently in the state's history, is preserved as a museum and library.

Many of New Mexico's state parks are results of man's ability to create lakes in the midst of an arid land. In the northwest area of the state, Navajo Dam State Park has been created by impounding the waters of the San Juan River. A storage reservoir on the Chama River centers El Vado State Park, and Bluewater Lake resulted from a dam on the Zuñi Mountain watershed. In Taos, Kit Carson State Park is a memorial to, and final resting place of, New Mexico's famous hero.

In northeastern New Mexico, Conchas Dam State Park is a product of the dam on the Canadian River. Tucumcari Metropolitan Park provides an excellent view of the bluffs of the Llano Estacado. Storrie Lake State Park is near Santa Fe, and Hyde Memorial State Park provides a recreational facility for the Santa Fe area. In the southeastern area of the state, parks are few. Oasis State Park is the site of shifting sand dunes near Portales. Bottomless Lakes State Park is an area of of great natural beauty a short distance east of Roswell. The state park at Lincoln is of historical interest.

The southwestern portion of New Mexico has large reservoirs on the Río Grande which lie in state parks at Elephant Butte and Caballo Lake. City of Rocks State Park near Deming is the site of unusual rock formations. Pancho Villa State Park at Columbus is a historical site with a botanical garden. La Mesilla State Park is of historical interest.

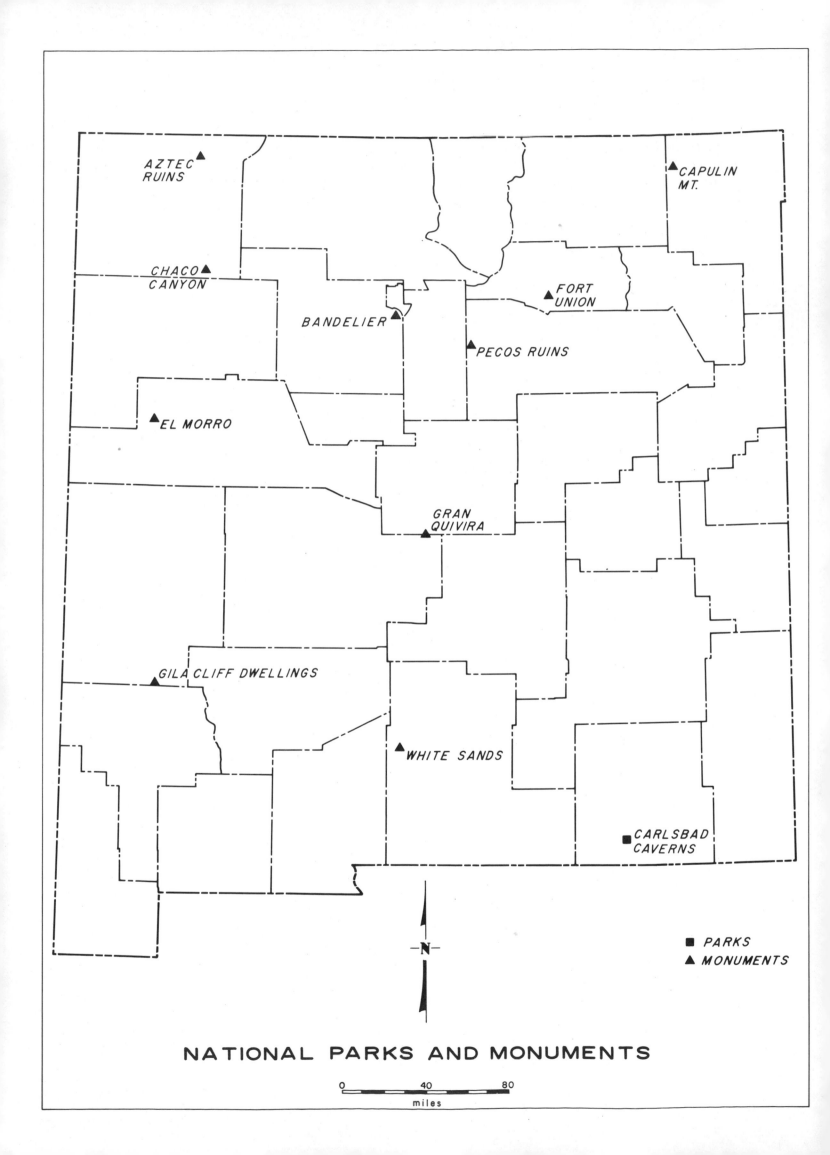

AZTEC
RUINS

▲ CAPULIN
MT.

CHACO
CANYON

▲ FORT
UNION

BANDELIER

▲ PECOS RUINS

▲ EL MORRO

GRAN
QUIVIRA

GILA CLIFF DWELLINGS

▲ WHITE SANDS

■ CARLSBAD
CAVERNS

■ PARKS
▲ MONUMENTS

—N—

NATIONAL PARKS AND MONUMENTS

0   40   80
miles

61. NATIONAL PARKS AND MONUMENTS

New Mexico has a historic past, is rich in archaeological remains, and has many unique geological features. This combination has helped develop its tourist industry. To preserve the heritage of the past and make it accessible to as many people as possible, the National Park Service of the United States Department of the Interior administers many parks and monuments within the state.

Easily the most important geological attraction of the state, and unique among the natural phenomena in the world, are the Carlsbad Caverns. Only a short distance away in the Tularosa Basin of south-central New Mexico is the White Sands National Monument. This, the world's largest gypsum desert, has drawn thousands of visitors because of its dazzling white dunes and their intriguing patterns of light and shadow. Capulin Mountain National Monument is one of the largest and most nearly symmetrical of the geologically recent cinder cones in the United States. It was formed by volcanic activity 7,000 years ago.

New Mexico has many spectacular ruins of prehistoric civilizations. One of these, Aztec Ruins National Monument, was the site of one of the largest pre-Spanish villages in the Southwest, from about A.D. 1100 to 1300. Associated with the Aztec ruins and dating from about the same time is Chaco Canyon National Monument. Contained in an area about two miles wide and eight miles long are a dozen great ruins and more than 300 smaller archaeological sites. The pueblo ruins of Bandelier National Monument date from about the twelfth to the sixteenth century and may have been established by Indians fleeing from Chaco Canyon. Besides archaeological sites, the area has superb natural scenery. The Gila Cliff Dwellings were six naturally formed caves in the face of a cliff, inhabited from A.D. 1100 to 1350. Some of the structures within Gran Quivira date back to A.D. 800, although its most significant period was from 1100 to 1400. The Spanish named it Pueblo de las Humanas. It was abandoned in the late seventeenth century.

More recent historical sites that have been preserved include the Pecos National Monument. Its Indian inhabitants date back to A.D. 1300, and the site was not abandoned until 1838. Fort Union was the largest military installation in the Southwest from 1851 to 1891, and the national monument which preserves its ruins is an impressive memorial to the men who won the West. El Morro is a massive mesapoint of sandstone that makes an impressive landmark. It is preserved for its record left by travelers as they passed. In fact, it is also known as "Inscription Rock."

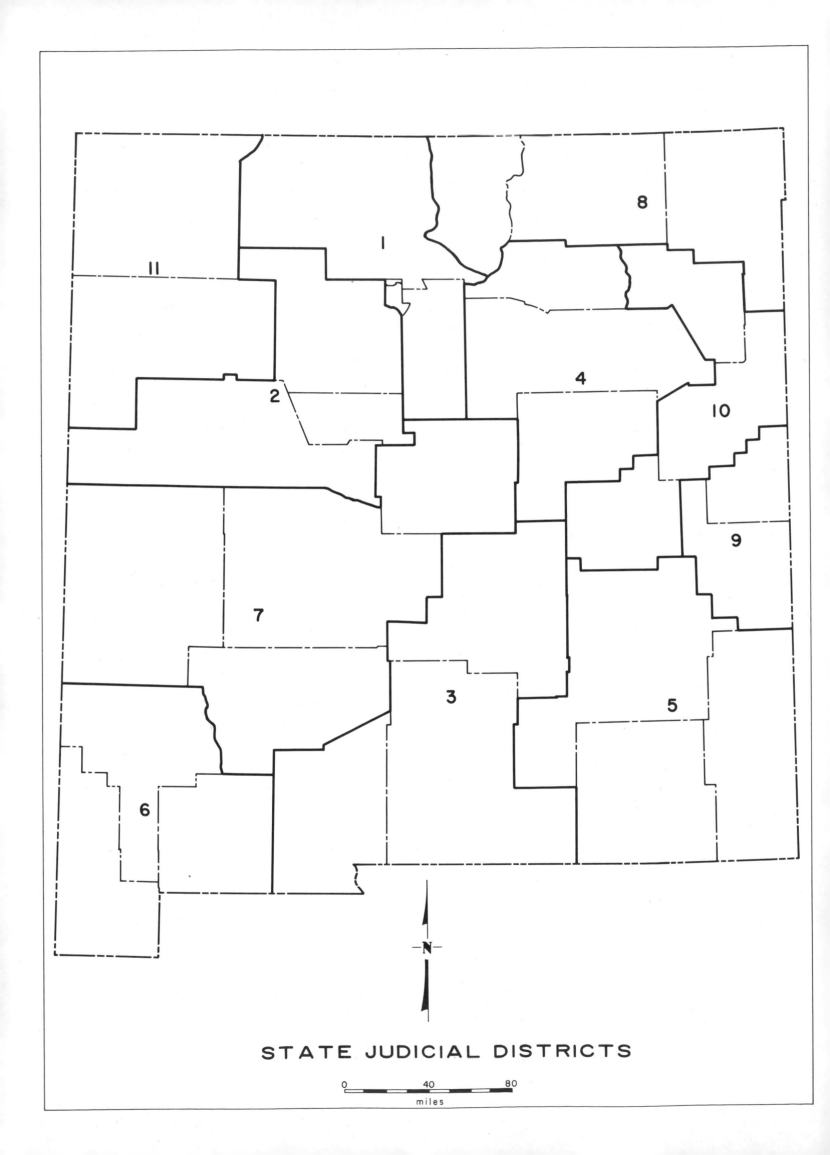

STATE JUDICIAL DISTRICTS

0   40   80
miles

62. STATE JUDICIAL DISTRICTS

NEW MEXICO has eleven state judicial districts. The original number has slowly increased through the years and the size of the districts has been altered as the state's population has grown. When it was first organized as a territory in 1851, the three judicial districts established by General Kearny in 1846 were retained. A fourth was added in 1887, a fifth in 1890, a sixth in 1904, and a seventh in 1909. Eight districts were authorized by the state constitution, a ninth added in 1921, a tenth in 1951, and the eleventh in 1961.

The effort to bring law and order to New Mexico sorely taxed the talents of the early jurists. There were far too few law enforcement officers, trained lawyers, and judges, for that matter. There were practically no jails, and far too many men were ready to challenge any kind of law. To New Mexico came those who chafed under the restraints of more civilized communities or were forced to flee from the law in Colorado or Texas.

In some ways New Mexico was like other American frontier communities, but in many respects the New Mexico frontier was different from others in America. Here an American frontier society was superimposed upon a Mexican frontier society, and the combination made the condition of general lawlessness extreme. This is not to imply that the native element was alone responsible for the general acceptability of criminality. Early visitors to Santa Fe frequently commented upon the fact that serious crimes were conspicuous by their absence among the Spanish-speaking people. Petty thievery was common, usually motivated by poverty. In southern and western New Mexico, a more typically American frontier society developed, but lawlessness was as widespread there as in the more preponderantly Spanish-American communities. In fact, research on the "outstanding" gunmen or outlaws of this period turns up very few Hispanic names.

Many travelers through the territory reported on the extensive lawlessness, and early jurists who tried cases in both territorial and federal courts despaired of ever taming the citizenry. The apogee of lawlessness was reached with the infamous Lincoln County War in the 1870's. It was near the end of the territorial period before law and order prevailed in New Mexico.

REFERENCES

REFERENCES are listed for individual maps. Publication information is given in the first listing of each book and is not repeated in subsequent references.

Map 1. Location of New Mexico

Espenshade, Edward B., Jr. (ed.) *Goode's World Atlas*, Eleventh Edition (Chicago, 1960).

Miller, Joseph (ed.), *New Mexico: A Guide to the Colorful State* (New York, 1940, 1953).

National Geographic Atlas of the Fifty States (Washington, 1960).

New Mexico Board of Development, Assorted Pamphlets (Santa Fe, various years).

Map 2. Landforms

Fenneman, Nevin M., *Physiography of Western United States* (New York, 1931).

Gordon, B. Leroy, Tuan Yi-Fu, *et al., Regions of New Mexico* (Albuquerque, 1961).

Map 3. Average Annual Precipitation

Gordon, *et al., Regions of New Mexico.*

United States Department of Commerce, "Reports of Weather Bureau Stations" (Various New Mexico stations, various years).

Ward, Robert DeCourcy, *The Climates of the United States* (Boston, 1925).

Map 4. Life Zones of Native Vegetation

Bailey, Vernon, *Life Zones and Crop Zones of New Mexico* (Washington, 1913).

New Mexico College of Agriculture and Mechanic Arts, *Vegetative Type Map of New Mexico* (Las Cruces, 1957).

Map 5. Drainage

Fenneman, *Physiography of Western United States.*

Harper, Allan G., Andrew R. Cordova, and Kalervo Obert, *Resources in the Middle Rio Grande Valley* (Albuquerque, 1943).

State of New Mexico, *Biennial Reports of the State Engineer* (Santa Fe, various years).

United States Geological Survey, *Mineral and Water Resources of New Mexico*, Bulletin No. 87 (Socorro, 1965).

Map 6. Game Fauna

Bailey, *Life Zones and Crop Zones of New Mexico.*

Bureau of Land Management, *Hunting and Fishing Map, New Mexico* (Santa Fe, n.d.).

Lang, E. Mickey, *Deer of New Mexico*, Bulletin No. 5 (New Mexico Department of Game and Fish, Santa Fe, 1957).

———, *Elk of New Mexico*, Bulletin No. 8 (New Mexico Department of Game and Fish, Santa Fe, 1958).

Miller, *New Mexico: A Guide.*

Spain, Larry, "Safari in Your Own Backyard," *Desert Magazine*, Vol. XXIX (January, 1966), 23–26.

Map 7. Average Number of Days Without Killing Frost

Gordon, *et al., Regions of New Mexico.*

State of New Mexico, *Biennial Reports of the State Engineer.*

United States Department of Commerce, "Weather Bureau Reports."

Ward, *Climates of the United States.*

Map 8. Mineral Resources—I & II

Anderson, Eugene Carter, *The Metal Resources of New Mexico and Their Economic Features Through 1954* (Socorro, 1957).

Edgel, Ralph, "Mining in New Mexico," *New Mexico Business*, Vol. XII (August, 1958).

Meaders, Margaret, "Copper Chronicle: The Story of New Mexico's 'Red Gold,'" *New Mexico Business*, Vol. XII (May and June, 1958).

Northrop, Stuart A., *Minerals of New Mexico* (Albuquerque, 1959).

Pearson, Jim Berry, "A New Mexico Gold Story—The Elizabethtown–Red River Area" (unpublished doctoral dissertation, University of Texas, 1955).

United States Department of the Interior, Bureau of Mines, *Minerals Yearbook* (Washington, various years).

United States Geological Survey, *Mineral and Water Resources of New Mexico.*

Map 9. Mineral Resources—III & IV

Anderson, *Metal Resources of New Mexico.*

New Mexico Bureau of Mines and Mineral Resources, *New Mexico Energy Resources Map* (Socorro, 1958).

Northrop, *Minerals of New Mexico.*

U.S. Bureau of Mines, *Mineral Yearbook.*

United States Geological Survey, *Mineral and Water Resources of New Mexico.*

Map 10. Mineral Resources—V & VI

Anderson, *Metal Resources of New Mexico.*

Bureau of Mines, *Minerals Yearbook.*

Kurrelmeyer, Louis H., *The Potash Industry* (Albuquerque, 1951).

New Mexico Bureau of Mines, *New Mexico Energy Resources Map.*

Northrop, *Minerals of New Mexico.*

United States Geological Survey, *Mineral and Water Resources of New Mexico.*

Map 11. Agriculture

Gordon, *et al., Regions of New Mexico.*

Irion, Frederick C. (ed.), *New Mexico and Its Natural Resources, 1900–2000* (Albuquerque, 1959).

New Mexico Department of Agriculture, *New Mexico Agricultural Statistics,* V (Las Cruces, 1966).

Water Resources Research Institute and Agricultural Experiment Station, *Map of Location of Irrigated Lands and Source of Water Areas of Similar Consumptive Use Factors in New Mexico* (New Mexico State University, Las Cruces, 1958).

Map 12. Sites of Prehistoric Civilizations

Gladwin, Harold S., *A History of the Ancient Southwest* (Portland, Maine, 1957).

Hewett, Edgar L., *Ancient Life in the American Southwest* (Indianapolis, 1930).

Hibben, Frank C., *The Lost Americans* (New York, 1946).

———, "Following the Trail of the First Americans," *New Mexico Magazine,* Vol. XLIV (October, 1966), 7–9, 34.

Kidder, Alfred Vincent, *An Introduction to the Study of Southwestern Archaeology* (New Haven, 1924, 1962).

Wormington, H. M., *Prehistoric Indians of the Southwest* (Denver Museum of Natural History, Popular Series No. 7, Denver, 1959).

Map 13. Spanish Expeditions: Sixteenth Century—I

Bishop, Morris, *The Odyssey of Cabeza de Vaca* (New York, 1933).

Bolton, Herbert E., *Coronado, Knight of Pueblo and Plains* (New York, 1949).

Day, A. Grove, *Coronado's Quest: The Discovery of the Southwestern States* (Berkeley, 1940).

Hammond, George P., and Agapito Rey, *Narratives of the Coronado Expedition, 1540–1542* (Albuquerque, 1940).

Map 14. Spanish Expeditions: Sixteenth Century—II

De Luxán, Pérez, *Expedition into New Mexico Made by Antonio de Espejo, 1582–1583,* trans. and ed. by George P. Hammond and Agapito Rey (Los Angeles, 1929).

De Sosa, Gaspar Castáno, *A Colony on the Move,* trans. and ed. by Albert H. Schroeder and Dan S. Matson (Santa Fe, 1956).

Hammond, George P., and Agapito Rey (eds. and trans.), *The Gallegos Relation of the Rodríguez Expedition* (Santa Fe, 1927).

———, *The Rediscovery of New Mexico, 1580–1594* (Albuquerque, 1966).

Mechem, J. Lloyd, "Antonio de Espejo and His Journey to New Mexico," *Southwestern Historical Quarterly,* Vol. XXX (October, 1926), 114–38.

———, "The Second Spanish Expedition to New Mexico," *New Mexico Historical Review,* Vol. I (April, 1926), 265–91.

Map 15. Pueblos and Nomadic Tribes, 1541

Bancroft, Hubert H., *Native Races,* 5 vols., I (San Francisco, 1886).

Bolton, *Coronado, Knight of Pueblo and Plains.*

Coolidge, Mary Roberts, *The Rain Makers: Indians of Arizona and New Mexico* (Boston, 1929).

Hodge, Frederick Webb, *Handbook of Indians North of Mexico,* 2 vols. (Washington, 1907, 1912).

Hyde, George E., *Indians of the High Plains* (Norman, 1959).

Jones, Oakah L., *Pueblo Warriors and Spanish Conquest* (Norman, 1966).

Sauer, Carl O., "The Distribution of Aboriginal Tribes and Languages in Northwestern Mexico," in *Ibero-Americana: 5* (Berkeley, 1934).

Map 16. Conquest, Pueblo Revolt, and Reconquest

Bailey, Jessie Bromilow, *Diego de Vargas and the Reconquest of New Mexico* (Albuquerque, 1940).

Chavez, Fray Angelico, "Pohe-Yemo's Representative and the Pueblo Revolt of 1680," *New Mexico Historical Review,* Vol. XLII (April, 1967), 85–126.

Espinosa, J. Manuel, *Crusaders of the Rio Grande* (Chicago, 1942).

Hackett, Charles W., "Retreat of the Spaniards from New Mexico in 1680, and the Beginnings of El Paso," *Southwestern Historical Quarterly,* Vol. XVI (October, 1912; December, 1912), 137–68.

———, "The Revolt of the Pueblo Indians of New Mexico in 1680," *Texas State Historical Quarterly,* Vol. XV (October, 1911), 93–147.

Hammond, George P., *Don Juan de Oñate and the Founding of New Mexico* (Santa Fe, 1927).

Map 17. First Towns

Bancroft, Hubert H. *History of Arizona and New Mexico, 1530–1888* (San Francisco, 1889).

Hackett, "Revolt of the Pueblo Indians in 1680."

Reeve, Frank, *History of New Mexico*, 2 vols., I (New York, 1961).

Map 18. Spanish-Mexican Expeditions

Bancroft, *Arizona and New Mexico, 1530–1888*.

Creer, Leland Hargrove, "Spanish-American Slave Trade in the Great Basin, 1800–1853," *New Mexico Historical Review*, Vol. XXIV (July, 1949), 171–84.

Hammond, George P., "The Zuniga Journal, Tucson to Santa Fe," *New Mexico Historical Review*, Vol. VI (January, 1931), 40–55.

Hill, Joseph J., "Spanish and Mexican Exploration and Trade Northwest from New Mexico into the Great Basin, 1765–1853," *Utah Historical Quarterly*, Vol. III (January, 1930), 3–23.

Reeve, *History of New Mexico*, I.

Map 19. The Boundaries of New Mexico During the Spanish and Mexican Periods

Baldwin, Percy M., "A Historical Note on the Boundaries of New Mexico," *New Mexico Historical Review*, Vol. V (April, 1930), 117–37.

Bancroft, *Arizona and New Mexico, 1530–1888*.

———, *History of the North Mexican States and Texas*, I, II (San Francisco, 1889).

Bowden, J. J., "The Texas–New Mexico Boundary Dispute Along the Rio Grande," *Southwestern Historical Quarterly*, Vol. LXIII (April, 1960), 221–37.

Map 20. Principal Towns and Road, 1800

Bancroft, *Arizona and New Mexico, 1530–1888*.

Moorhead, Max L., *New Mexico's Royal Road: Trade and Travel on the Chihuahua Trail* (Norman, 1958).

Reeve, *History of New Mexico*, I.

Map 21. Spanish Land Grants

Bancroft, *Arizona and New Mexico, 1530–1888*.

Bureau of Land Management, *State of New Mexico*, Provisional Edition (Santa Fe, 1963).

Fitzgerrell, J. J., "An Open Letter to President Cleveland," (Broadside in Huntington Library, San Marino, California, Las Vegas, New Mexico, 1886).

Poldervaart, Arie W., *Black-Robed Justice* (Albuquerque, 1948).

Ritch, William Gillette, Collected Papers of, in Huntington Library, San Marino, California.

Twitchell, Ralph Emerson, *The Leading Facts of New Mexican History*, 2 vols., II (Albuquerque, 1912, 1963).

Map 22. Nomadic Tribes circa 1845

Reeve, *History of New Mexico*, I.

Simpson, James H., "Map of the Route pursued in 1849 by the U.S. Troops under the command of Bvt. Lieut. Col. Jno. M. Washington, Governor of New Mexico," in *An Expedition Against the Navaho Indians* (Santa Fe, 1849).

Smith, Anne M., *New Mexico Indians* (Santa Fe, 1966).

Sonnichsen, C. L., *The Mescalero Apaches* (Norman, 1958).

Thomas, Alfred B., *The Chiricahua Apache, 1695–1876* (Albuquerque, 1959).

———, *The Mescalero Apache, 1653–1874* (Albuquerque, 1959).

Warren, Gouverneur K., "Map of the Territory of the United States from the Mississippi River to the Pacific Ocean," in *Reports of Explorations and Surveys, to ascertain the most practicable and economical route for a Railroad from the Mississippi River to the Pacific Ocean, H.R. Ex. Doc. 91,* Vol. XI, 33 Cong., 2 sess. (Washington, 1854).

Wilson, John P., *Military Campaigns in the Navajo Country* (Santa Fe, 1967).

Map 23. Anglo-American Expeditions Before 1846

Abert, James W., and William G. Peck, "Map showing the route pursued by the exploring expedition to New Mexico and the southern Rocky Mountains . . . during the year 1845," in U.S. 29 Cong., 1 sess., 1845–1846, *Sen. Doc. 438* (Washington, 1846).

Bancroft, *Arizona and New Mexico, 1530–1888*.

Bender, Averam B., "Government Explorations in the Territory of New Mexico 1846–1859," *New Mexico Historical Review*, Vol. IX (January, 1934), 1–32.

Duncan, Robert Lipscomb, *Reluctant General: The Life and Times of Albert Pike* (New York, 1961).

Hollon, W. Eugene, *The Lost Pathfinder: Zebulon Montgomery Pike* (Norman, 1949).

Loomis, Noel M., *The Texan–Santa Fé Pioneers* (Norman, 1958).

Tucker, John M., "Major Long's Route from the Arkansas to the Canadian River, 1830," *New Mexico Historical Review*, Vol. XXXVIII (July, 1963), 185–219.

Map 24. United States Military Expeditions During the Mexican War

Bender, "Government Explorations in the Territory of New Mexico."

Clarke, Dwight L., *Stephen Watts Kearny, Soldier of the West* (Norman, 1961).

Edwards, Frank S., *A Campaign in New Mexico with Colonel Doniphan* (Philadelphia, 1847).

Emory, William H., "Notes of a Military Reconnoissance from Fort Leavenworth, in Missouri to San Diego, in California," *Ex. Doc. 41,* 30 Cong. 1 sess. (Washington, 1848).

Gibson, George R., *Journal of a Soldier Under Kearny*

and Doniphan, 1846–1847 (Glendale, California, 1935).

Hughes, John T., Doniphan's Expedition (Cincinnati, 1848).

Ruhlen, George, "Kearny's Route from the Rio Grande to the Gila River," New Mexico Historical Review, Vol. XXXII (July, 1957), 213–30.

Tyler, Daniel, A Concise History of the Mormon Battalion in the Mexican War 1846–1848 (Chicago, 1881).

Map 25. United States Military Expeditions
After the Mexican War

Bender, "Government Explorations in the Territory of New Mexico."

Reeve, History of New Mexico, II.

Map 26. The Treaty of Guadalupe Hidalgo
Boundary Dispute

Baldwin, "Historical Note on the Boundaries of New Mexico."

Disturnell, J., "Mapa de los Estados Unidos de Mejico" (Treaty Map, 1847, New York).

Hammond, George P. (ed.), The Treaty of Guadalupe Hidalgo, February Second, 1848 (San Francisco, 1949).

Rittenhouse, Jack, The Story of Disturnell's Treaty Map (Santa Fe, 1965).

Map 27. Principal Towns and Cart Roads, 1850

Bancroft, Arizona and New Mexico, 1530–1888.

Moorhead, New Mexico's Royal Road.

Reeve, History of New Mexico, II.

United States Bureau of the Census, U.S. Census of Population: 1850 (Washington, 1850).

Map 28. The Gadsden Purchase, 1853

Garber, Paul N., The Gadsden Purchase (Philadelphia, 1923).

Rippy, J. Fred, The United States and Mexico (New York, 1926).

Map 29. Territory of New Mexico, 1850–1861

Bancroft, Arizona and New Mexico, 1530–1888.

Reeve, History of New Mexico, II.

Twitchell, Ralph E., Leading Facts of New Mexican History, II.

Wylls, Arthur S., A History of Arizona (Phoenix, 1950).

Map 30. The Texas Claim After the Conclusion
of Peace with Mexico

Baldwin, "Historical Note on the Boundaries of New Mexico."

Binkley, William Campbell, "The Question of Texan Jurisdiction in New Mexico Under the United States 1844–1850," Southwestern Historical Quarterly, Vol. XXIV (July, 1920), 1–38.

Bowden, "The Texas–New Mexico Boundary Dispute Along the Rio Grande."

Ganaway, Loomis Morton, New Mexico and the Sectional Controversy (Albuquerque, 1944).

Map 31. Proposed Division of New Mexico, 1857

Baldwin, "A Historical Note on the Boundaries of New Mexico."

Reeve, History of New Mexico, II.

Wylls, History of Arizona.

Map 32. Division of New Mexico

Baldwin, "Historical Note on the Boundaries of New Mexico."

U.S. Boundary Commission, New Mexico v. Colorado, No. 1 (Original, October Term, 1960).

Reeve, History of New Mexico, II.

Remley, Helen M., "Cadastral Surveys" (manuscript in Bureau Land Management Office, Santa Fe, n.d.).

Wylls, History of Arizona.

Map 33. Principal Meridian and Base Line

Bureau of Land Management, Map, State of New Mexico, provisional edition (Santa Fe, 1963).

"Field Notes, New Mexican Principal Meridian, established by John W. Garretson, Deputy Surveyor, under contract number 1 bearing date March 9, 1855, William Pelham, United States Surveyor General" (manuscript in Survey Records Section, Bureau of Land Management, Santa Fe).

Haase, Ynez D., "The Mapping of New Mexico, 1805–1890," (unpublished manuscript).

New Mexico State Highway Department, Quadrangle Maps of the State of New Mexico (Santa Fe, 1962).

Reeve, History of New Mexico, II.

Map 34. Historic Trails

Bender, Averam B., "Military Transportation in the Southwest, 1848, 1860," New Mexico Historical Review, Vol. XXXII (April, 1957), 123–50.

Gregg, Josiah, Commerce of the Prairies, ed. by Max L. Moorhead (Norman, 1954).

Hafen, LeRoy, and Ann, The Old Spanish Trail (Glendale, California, 1955).

Haley, J. Evetts, "The Comanchero Trade," Southwestern Historical Quarterly, Vol. XXXVIII (January, 1935), 157–76.

Lawrence, Eleanor, "Mexican Trade Between Santa Fe and Los Angeles," California Historical Quarterly, Vol. X (March, 1931), 27–39.

Moorhead, New Mexico's Royal Road.

Winther, Oscar Osburn, "The Southern Overland Mail and Stagecoach Line 1857–1861," New Mexico Historical Review, Vol. XXXII (April, 1957), 81–106.

Map 35. United States Military Forts

Bender, Averam B., "Frontier Defense in the Territory of New Mexico, 1846–1853," *New Mexico Historical Review*, Vol. IX (July, 1934), 249–72; (October, 1934), 345–73.

Frazer, Robert W., *Forts of the West* (Norman, 1965).

Hart, Herbert M., *Old Forts of the Southwest* (Seattle, 1964).

Kelly, Lawrence C., "Where Was Fort Canby?" *New Mexico Historical Review*, Vol. XLII (January, 1967), 49–61.

Prucha, Francis Paul, *A Guide to the Military Posts of the United States, 1789–1895* (Madison, 1964).

Ruth, Kent, *Great Day in the West: Forts, Posts, and Rendezvous Beyond the Mississippi* (Norman, 1963).

Map 36. Military Operations During the Civil War, 1862

Colton, Ray C., *The Civil War in the Western Territories* (Norman, 1959).

Ganaway, Loomis Morton, *New Mexico and the Sectional Controversy* (Albuquerque, 1944).

Keleher, William A., *Turmoil in New Mexico: 1846–1868* (Santa Fe, 1952).

Kerby, Robert L., *The Confederate Invasion of New Mexico, 1861–1862* (Los Angeles, 1958).

United States War Department, *The War of the Rebellion. A Compilation of the Official Records of the Union and Confederate Armies*, Series 1, Vol. XXXIV, Part 1. Also the *Atlas* (Washington, 1880–1901).

Map 37. The Battle of Valverde, 1862; the Battle of Glorieta Pass, 1862

Colton, *The Civil War in the Western Territories*.

Keleher, *Turmoil in New Mexico: 1846–1868*.

Kerby, *Confederate Invasion of New Mexico, 1861–1862*.

United States War Department, *War of the Rebellion*.

Map 38. Indian and American Military Engagements, 1848–1886

Bennett, James A., *Forts and Forays* (Albuquerque, 1948).

Carson, Kit, *Kit Carson's Autobiography* (Lincoln, n.d.).

Davis, Britton, *The Truth About Geronimo* (New Haven, 1963).

Dunn, Jacob Piatt, Jr., *Massacres of the Mountains* (New York, n.d.).

Etsedi, Peshlakai, " 'The Long Walk' to Bosque Redondo," *Museum Notes* (Museum of Northern Arizona, Flagstaff, May, 1937).

Sonnichsen, *Mescalero Apaches*.

Thomas, *Chiricahua Apache*.

———, *Mescalero Apache*.

Wallace, Ernest, and Adamson Hoebel, *The Comanches* (Norman, 1952).

Map 39. Cattle Trails, 1866–1880

Dale, Edward Everett, *The Range Cattle Industry* (Norman, 1930).

Haley, J. Evetts, *Charles Goodnight, Cowman and Plainsman* (Norman, 1949).

———, *The XIT Ranch of Texas and the Early Days of the Llano Estacado* (Norman, 1953).

Hinton, Harwood Perry, Jr., "John Simpson Chisum, 1877–1884," (unpublished master's thesis, Columbia University, 1956).

Love, Clara M., "History of the Cattle Industry in the Southwest," *Southwestern Historical Quarterly*, Vol. XIX (April, July, 1916), 370–99.

Raine, William MacLeod, *Cattle, Cowboys and Rangers* (New York, 1930).

Richardson, Rupert N., and Carl Coke Rister, *The Greater Southwest* (Glendale, California, 1934).

Map 40. Stagecoach Lines

Wallace, William S., "Short-Line Staging in New Mexico," *New Mexico Historical Review*, Vol. XXVI (April, 1951), 89–100.

———, "Stagecoaching in Territorial New Mexico," *New Mexico Historical Review*, Vol. XXXII (April, 1957), 204–10.

Maps 41–52. County Boundary Changes

The basic source for the county structure of New Mexico is still Charles F. Coan, "The County Boundaries of New Mexico," *Southwestern Political Science Quarterly*, Vol. III (December, 1922), 252–86; reprinted in Santa Fe, 1965.

Map 53. Principal Towns and Railroads, 1890

Bancroft, *Arizona and New Mexico, 1530–1888*.

Greever, William S., "Railway Development in the Southwest," *New Mexico Historical Review*, Vol. XXXII (April, 1957), 151–203.

Reeve, *History of New Mexico*, II.

United States Bureau of the Census, *U.S. Census of Population: 1890* (Washington, D.C., 1890).

Map 54. Principal Cities and Roads, 1930

Edgel, Ralph L., "New Mexico Population: Its Size and Its Changing Distribution," *New Mexico Business*, Vol. XII (October, 1958).

New Mexico State Highway Department, Highway Map, 1930 (Santa Fe).

United States Bureau of the Census, *U.S. Census of Population: 1930*.

Map 55. Principal Cities and Roads, 1960

Edgel, "New Mexico Population: Its Size and Its Changing Distribution."

New Mexico State Highway Department (Santa Fe, various maps).

United States Bureau of the Census, *U.S. Census of Population: 1960*, Vol. I, *Characteristics of the Population*, Part A, "Number of Inhabitants."

Map 56. Indian Tribal Lands

Bureau of Indian Affairs, Department of the Interior, *Indians of New Mexico Today* (Washington, D.C., 1966).

Dale, Edward Everett, *Indians of the Southwest* (Norman, 1949).

Smith, Anne M., *New Mexico Indians*.

Sonnichsen, *Mescalero Apaches*.

Map 57. Present Indian Pueblo Towns

Bureau of Indian Affairs, *Indians of New Mexico Today*.

Jones, *Pueblo Warriors and Spanish Conquest*.

Schroeder, Albert H., "The Language of the Saline Pueblos Piro or Tiwa?" *New Mexico Historical Review*, Vol. XXXIX (July, 1964), 235–50.

Smith, *New Mexico Indians*.

Stubbs, Stanley A., *Bird's-Eye View of the Pueblos* (Norman, 1950).

Map 58. Railroads: 1878–1966

Boatwright, C. C., *Transportation and Communications in New Mexico* (State Planning Office, Santa Fe, 1966).

Greever, "Railway Development in the Southwest."

Map 59. National Forests

Surveys and Maps Branch, Division of Engineering, *U.S. Forest Service, Establishment and Modification of National Forest Boundaries, a Chronological Record, 1891–1962* (Washington, D.C., 1962).

Map 60. State Parks and Monuments

Miller, *New Mexico: A Guide*.

Tourist Division, Department of Development, State of New Mexico (Santa Fe, various publications).

Map 61. National Parks and Monuments

National Park Service, United States Department of Interior (various publications).

Map 62. State Judicial Districts

New Mexico Blue Book, 1965–1966 (Santa Fe).

Otero, Miguel, *My Life on the Frontier*, I (New York, 1935–39).

Poldervaart, *Black-Robed Justice*.

Reeve, *History of New Mexico*, II.

INDEX